Practical Mysticism

Practical Mysticism

by
Edward Lee

AMORC

Published by the Grand Lodge of the English
Language Jurisdiction, AMORC, Inc.
1342 Naglee Avenue, San Jose, CA 95191
www.rosicrucian.org

©2012, 2005, Supreme Grand Lodge of the Ancient & Mystical Order Rosae Crucis
Published by the Grand Lodge of the English Language Jurisdiction, AMORC, Inc.

ISBN 1-893971-11-2

Library of Congress Control Number: 2005931353

10 9 8 7 6 5 4 3 2 1

Printed and bound in U.S.A.

Table of Contents

Foreword

While reading the chapters of this book, you may wonder about several key words—such as *mystic, mysticism,* the *Cosmic,* and *God*—that you may have never come across before, or are used in a way that is new to you. Since the specific meaning of these terms may elude you, I wish to take this opportunity to provide the following explanations that I believe will shed some light on these subjects.

Mystic and mysticism—have there ever been two words so misunderstood and maligned by various writers? *Mysticism* does not refer to anything mysterious. It is not mystery. Mysticism is simply the process by which an individual may experience direct, conscious union with the Absolute, Divine Mind, Universal Intelligence, or what Rosicrucian students refer to as the *God of their Hearts.* It is the intimate and direct awareness of God or the Cosmic through Self, that is, through the domain of the subconscious. This doesn't happen by adhering to specific tenets or beliefs, but by learning and applying natural laws that, over time, allow students to experience consciousness of the Cosmic.

What is the *Cosmic?* It is the divine, infinite intelligence of the Supreme Being permeating everything. It is the totality of laws and phenomena that manifests throughout nature—and therefore throughout humanity—all the forces, energies, and powers that account for the finite and infinite worlds.

The *mystic*, then, is the student, the knowledge-seeker, who through the process of studying mysticism seeks direct, conscious union with Universal Intelligence and the Cosmic. Perhaps former Rosicrucian Imperator H. Spencer Lewis best defined the mystic when he wrote the following: "What actually constitutes the mystic? Wherein is the true mystic so different from other earthly beings? What is the essence of mysticism that makes it so wonderful and so sacred at the same time? Is it not the conscious attunement with Divinity and the Cosmic which comes from the *knowledge and the ability to apply* and use the laws of God and nature constructively?"

A profound question which leads us to a good definition of the word *God*. Rosicrucians do not attempt to define the nature of deity, because each person finds this definition within his or her own heart. God is wholly a subjective experience and thus a personal interpretation. The concept of God reflects the intelligence, education, religious and social background of each individual. For these reasons it is impossible to create a uniform conception of God acceptable to all individuals alike. But most Rosicrucians feel there is but one God, ever-living, ever-present, without limiting attributes or definite form or manifestation—it is the *God of our Hearts*.

In this book, *Practical Mysticism*, author Edward Lee answers typical questions that have been asked of correspondents, instructors, and official representatives of the Rosicrucian Order, AMORC, over his thirty years of employment at the organization's headquarters in San Jose, California. The author points out that throughout those years his "answers and comments, as it turns out, were not exclusively relevant to students of mysticism but to many other persons who were serious about bettering their lives from the inside out. There is no doubt about the fact, however, that inner self-development is a slow and gradual process, but ultimately worth all the effort it takes to achieve it."

And so in this spirit of discovering workable answers to age-old questions, let us begin to learn about the practical application of mystical laws and principles in our everyday lives.

—*Robin M. Thompson, Editor*

"This above all:

to thine own

self be true...."

Chapter 1

Who Are You?

"In my life I have to please so many persons and under such a multitude of differing conditions, that I'm having trouble realizing the true nature of my own personality. I often ask myself: 'Who am I?'"

The plot of an unusual film of the 1940s, entitled *A Double Life*, centered upon a man known to his friends and critics as being a fine actor. In this dark and gripping movie, the actor is called upon to play the part of Shakespeare's tragic hero, Othello. So totally absorbed in the role of Othello does this man become that he begins to forget his own life outside of the theater as opposed to the life of Othello on stage. His tormented mind blurs the difference between actuality and play acting. He eventually loses complete control of himself and believes himself to be the jealous lover, Othello. In a rage, he subsequently commits a crime of passion one night, offstage. Since we know that Shakespeare's Othello takes his own life at the conclusion of the drama, the film, *A Double Life*, ends on a tragic note indeed.

In a less dramatic way, we often feel called upon in our daily lives to assume a "role," much as a performer on

11

stage. We may begin our day, for example, by playing the part of the parent. We continue our day as the commuter. We then become the worker or manager. If we attend classes at night, we are transformed into the student. Our weekends may find us acting the part of the sportsman or entertainer, or perhaps even the lover.

Taking into account the fact that each person has his or her own pattern of existence, each may see self in a variety of different roles and in a myriad of acting assignments, depending on the individual. The conviction and intensity with which we carry out these self-appointed roles also depend upon the performing ability of the individual. The reasons we do these things may also vary, but it is perhaps safe to say that we are attempting them for several reasons: to achieve a sense of purpose in life; to find psychological security and protect ourselves from the unexpected; or to maintain mental control over our environment and, most importantly, ourselves. Nevertheless, in spite of our ability to conform to differing social conditions, notwithstanding our will power and acting talents, an overriding sense of futility may still haunt us. In our quieter moments, like a giant sunken ship emerging from the depths, our real self may begin to present itself.

Such a superficial restriction as *society* may have dictated to us what we should say when we speak to our children and how we should act when we are with our spouse. Fear often restricts our attitude at our place of employment, while a *need for acceptance* tells us what we should do and think while among our friends. If our daily circumstances change in rapid enough succession, our role playing may resemble an old-style theatrical quick-change artist, frantically changing costumes.

For example, some years ago I was able to quietly observe a colleague in a variety of social and business situations. His kaleidoscopic personality changes were amazing. To his wife he was silent and reserved; to his children, rude and hostile; to his friends, a fun-loving comrade; to his employer, he was servile and meek; to the women on the job he was a gallant cavalier. However, one day during a moment of clear insight, I suddenly realized the real nature of this person. It came as a shock. I felt the loneliness and fear that radiated from him. I realized further that he was not totally unlike many other people— not unlike myself at that time. It was simply that role-playing was a more pronounced aspect of his character, whereas with most other persons it is partially hidden.

At times of such humbling self-awareness we wonder why we insist on living a life of duplicity. We are reminded of the words of a writer who said, "He was a chameleon and his rare capacity for recognizing what was required of him was equaled only by his capacity for becoming it." We may be struck by the fact that day in and day out, year after year, we often move about in a personally directed theatrical performance. We pretend; we play the role. *Why?* From what are we hiding? Which is the real personality and which is the charade?

Getting back to our confused actor and Othello, if we follow his example and the false face we assume is allowed to become our master, then pain is the inevitable result. That is to say, if we always permit our five physical senses to dictate to our inner selves as to how we will truly conduct our lives, then we are in effect throwing away our anchor in this often-turbulent sea of life. If our outer self has no conscious connection, no bridge to our inner being, then in a storm our ship has no safe port. The practical value of a rational study of mysticism and self-knowledge cannot be overestimated.

Authentic mystical teachings often refer to the evolving soul personality, the refinement of character, and the improvement of the whole being. These are not generalities but instead are fundamental reasons for the existence of such venerable organizations as the Rosicrucian Order, AMORC, and others. Each sincere student on the Path is not only unfolding the psychic centers, becoming more intuitive and shedding unwanted habits, but is also gradually realizing his or her place in life. It is gratifying to know that such students are in fact carving out for themselves a personal philosophy of life, one which will make them the happy and contented persons they long to be. We have observed that true mystical teachings are definitely not in the business of trying to make all of its students think exactly alike. They do not envision a giant mystical factory where, at the end of a conveyor belt, all students fall off the assembly line in a uniform way. They are not attempting to be like a cookie-cutter, but do encourage the serious student on to *independent* thought and applying what is learned in a practical way.

In this chapter, we have mentioned those who, for the most part, are unconsciously role-playing through life. Those who *consciously* do so in order to achieve a psychological dominance over the other person, or to outwit someone through duplicity and misrepresentation, are in another category entirely. The gaining of advantage through negative means gave birth to the delicious axiom: "Oh, what a tangled web we weave, when first we practice to deceive!"

It goes without saying that there are people who must practice duplicity as a matter of personal survival, as in the case of law enforcement operatives and those who do so in order to save lives in dangerous situations; also those who are professional performers, actors, and so on. In this discussion we are chiefly concerned with those who hide *from themselves* through an unconscious series of cloaks and masks so as not to face the truth about themselves as they really are.

So, what are the benefits of being honest with self, of courageously and gradually improving the personality? For one thing, it ultimately gives us an unshakeable sense of personal identity. There emerges a most agreeable feeling of being a unique person. For another, we become at ease with self and gradually cease the search for outward assurances from friends and neighbors, and become a friend and neighbor to ourselves.

A serious student of mysticism will hesitate to do anything that will interfere with or destroy the newly constructed inner connection. He or she becomes a more positive individual, free from a multitude of fears, one of those individuals who seems at ease under any circumstance.

We, in turn, feel at ease in their company, as they appear to have no counterfeit image of themselves with which they seek to impress others. They move among both the world-renowned and the humble poor with the same genuineness and sincerity, free of hypocrisy. They become an ideal toward which others can strive.

If you are looking for a guidepost in your search for self-identity and inner awakening, remember this relevant quotation from *Hamlet*:

This above all: to thine own self be true,
And it must follow, as the night the day,
Thou canst not then be false to any man.

"Concentration is...

the gathering,

the collecting of our

mental energy into

a single pinpoint

of undiluted,

intense force."

Chapter 2

The Ability to Concentrate

During an informal discussion at a Rosicrucian gathering in a large American city, a woman asked: "How does one finally go about achieving a greater success with all of these mental exercises that are written about in our lessons and practiced at home?"

It is a self-evident truth to say that a house should be built upon a firm foundation. When it comes to constructing a better, finer character and a more spiritual personality for ourselves, the foundation should consist of those conditions that are just as solid and strong. We refer to such things as aspiration, sincerity, goal setting, and the ability to *concentrate*. There are other ingredients that could justifiably be added to our abstract foundation, but at this time we wish to direct our attention exclusively to mystical concentration.

What is concentration? It is the bringing together and the directing of our thoughts to a common center. It is the gathering, the collecting of our mental energy into a single pinpoint of undiluted, intense force. For instance, when producing maple syrup, one concentrates the sap by boiling it. Milk that is to be vacuum packed in a can must be condensed by removing the water from it. By the same token, we render our wandering thoughts less dilute by willfully rejecting the extraneous. In fact, the word *concentrate* means something that is undiluted, condensed, and therefore increased in strength. Our concentrated thoughts automatically become a strong force, a potent power for good.

If you wish to see an excellent example of concentration, watch one of those documentary films about nature that shows a lioness stalking a zebra. You will observe the total silence, the menacing stealth, the hypnotic gaze, and the gathering of the animal body into one dynamic mass until this force and power is suddenly unleashed in a lightning strike of great intensity. This is purity of purpose demonstrated for us in a totally natural setting provided by nature.

When an artist is creating a work of art, such as a painting, he or she often enters into a mental state whereby all of the faculties are absorbed into the project in progress. The surface plane of consciousness, the objective level, begins receiving information from the deeper subjective mental arena, and certain imaginative impressions start to flow. Entering even deeper into concentration upon this work, the artist passes into a state of mind whereby subconscious mental input is possible. The subconscious, being the most profound level of consciousness, is in contact with the great Cosmic Mind, and inspirational ideas and impressions may flash across the threshold of the inner mind. Such ideas are then subjectively translated into useful thoughts and pictures that are perhaps added to the work of art. Such persons are often completely oblivious of their surroundings, and if another person were to suddenly burst into the artist's studio, that would cause the artist to be forcefully and abruptly brought back to the surface of consciousness. As a sidelight, it is the irritated reaction of an artist at such a time that may have originally given rise to the expression "temperamental artist."

In the example of the lioness, we witness the drawing together, the collecting of all physical and emotional forces into a common center of attention for accomplishing a single purpose. This is also true of the artist at work; here we see undiluted concentration. But among humans something much more vital is added, so let us consider what this is. As mystical students focus their thoughts on a higher concept or perhaps some special exercise, they then begin to move gradually closer to *attunement* with the Cosmic Mind. We will have more to say about this concept later.

There are people who say that they have no difficulty at all in concentrating, and perhaps they do not. However, such persons are few and far between. For most of us, the ability to concentrate is difficult to achieve and must be *developed* on a step-by-step basis. Like all other art forms, there are rules, guidelines, stages of development, and personal effort involved for progress to be made. Perhaps because of the widely available nature of instant entertainment these days, especially in the Western world, often young people are not called upon to discipline the mind and to mentally create, unless they are individually interested in such matters. That may be the reason today for such a wide proliferation of business seminars that offer to help adults train their minds and concentrate their thinking faculties, because success in business, as in mysticism, depends heavily upon the *ability to concentrate.*

Speaking of rules, what are some suggestions for students to follow in order to improve their ability to concentrate? First, one must have a *purpose* for concentrating. When we speak of a purpose, we mean primarily a single purpose. In other words, if the mind is cluttered with six or seven conflicting ideas and goals, very little of a beneficial nature will be forthcoming from a period of concentration. Therefore, at this point, we begin figuratively to boil the water from the milk or condense the sap to make syrup. We make our thoughts more intense and powerful. If, for example, we wish to conduct a special exercise and concentrate on all parts of the body, we must discard all stray thoughts of what happened on the job today, or what we plan to have for lunch tomorrow, and so on. Then, like a beam of light that searches out and focuses on a single spot only, we shine our thoughts on one part of the body at a time and imagine energy and glowing health in that area; we feel that area tingle and the energy move slowly up until we encompass our entire body with our thoughts.

Second, there should be present a motive for concentrating. The student should have an unselfish reason for wishing to accomplish a particular objective through concentration; otherwise the ultimate result will not be satisfactory to the student.

For example, suppose you wish to obtain a new home. You then proceed to concentrate and use all the correct techniques for mentally creating this new environment. However, inherent, incorporated, and deeply embedded in that mental plan for a new home should be the thought that once it is obtained, it is going to be used, at least partially, for the benefit of others. You may foresee a larger environment in which your children or perhaps grandchildren might visit from time to time. You may visualize more suitable rooms for accomplishing some worthwhile goal. For example, an artist may need a larger, quieter, better-lighted environment to create beauty for others to enjoy.

Third, tied in closely with your motive, is deservedness. In using the word *deserve*, we mean that enormous ebb and flow of Cosmic Law that permeates all nature and pulsates through our lives. For example, it may very well be that the home we are visualizing and concentrating upon with all our heart and soul may not actually be in our best interests to receive at this time, and the Cosmic will not cooperate and help bring about a manifestation the way we wish it to.

Before continuing, we must point out that this principle applies particularly to those mystical students who are sincerely interested in working harmoniously with the Cosmic Mind. In such cases it appears as though the Cosmic, instead of aiding students with their plans, does *not* assist in fruition. Students may be disappointed that their plans are not working out, but perhaps months or years later, they will look back and be eternally grateful to the Cosmic that these plans did not come about. "Man proposes and God disposes" may be another way of explaining deservedness.

To summarize: Discipline the mind; insist within that there will be but a *single* thought upon which you will focus your attention. Discard all extraneous and wandering thoughts that come to the mind. You will find that the power to accomplish such strong concentrated thought will gradually become easier as you practice this forceful focusing of the mind.

Next, we must be *unselfish*, at least to some degree, in the desire for success in mystical experimentation. Intrinsically wound up in the desire for success must be the willingness to be of some service to humanity.

The final stage of mystical concentration is where concentration ends and inner attunement becomes truly dominant. In other words, at this stage the student has already filtered out all useless thoughts and is working with a single objective only. The conscience is clear, and he or she has the correct attitude of humility. Next, the student should exercise force of will to dismiss the single thought and allow the subconscious mind freedom to receive intuitive impressions.

Up to this point, the student has been concentrating. However, when the student stops objective thinking, releases the thought while in that borderline state, he or she begins to *meditate*. In this context, attunement and meditation are synonymous terms. Some persons enter into this state of attunement without willfully attempting to do so, as in the case of the artist spoken of earlier. At such times, helpful and inspirational ideas often flash into consciousness, bringing with them a thrill of renewed enthusiasm and pleasure. Such ideas or impressions are ultimately practical and useful in daily life.

Therefore, it may seem contradictory to say this, but successful mystical concentration includes ultimately the ability to *stop* concentrating, and the willingness to submit within to the meditative state.

Finally, as far as utilizing the Rosicrucian ability to concentrate for such activities as thought transmission and related phenomena, authentic mystical tradition gives this definite precautionary advice:

> *The Cosmic will not carry your thoughts for any destructive, unfair, or unethical reason. There is no inexplicable magic in this; it is simply good, clean, honest transmission of thought power, and it needs the cooperation of the Cosmic to bring it about. The Cosmic will not help you do anything that will injure or hurt anyone.*

"The ways and means
by which we deal
with our problems
often have far-reaching
effects on our lives and
the lives of those
around us."

Chapter 3

Problem Solving

There are any number of reasons why we experience problems in our lives: a lack of understanding of a given situation; insufficent control of our emotions; overemphasis on one minor condition; underemphasis concerning a more serious matter; and so on. The ways and means by which we deal with our problems often have far-reaching effects on our lives and the lives of those around us.

We might say that a problem is an *unsettled* matter demanding a solution, or at least a decision. It is normally an issue that requires concentrated thought or personal skill for its satisfactory solution. It usually entails doubt, uncertainty, and sometimes fear. There are various kinds of problems, such as social problems, problem neighborhoods, or problem children. The type of problem that we will focus on in this discussion is personal problems and their means of solution, using mysticism as a practical tool for accomplishment.

Problem solving has become a basic kind of thinking and has received much study by psychologists and other students of human behavior, such as students of the

Rosicrucian Order. Problem solving activity falls broadly into two categories: one emphasizes simple trial and error; the other requires some degree of what is sometimes referred to as *insight*. The mystical connotations of this latter method shall be developed shortly.

In trial and error, the individual proceeds mainly by exploring and manipulating elements of the problem situation in an effort to sort out possibilities and to run across steps that might bring him or her closer to the goal in mind. Trial and error activity is not necessarily overt, as in one attempting to fit together pieces of a jigsaw puzzle. It may be you, as the one attempting to solve your problem, simply reflecting on the dilemma and mentally testing possibilities. You may put forth a certain amount of intellectual exertion aimed at finding an answer to your question, or at least a means of achieving a desirable, practical goal. You want peace and harmony to reign within, with respect to the particular problem you have in mind.

You may decide to resort to the method utilized in some research institutes—namely, the use of diagrams to assist you in seeing the whole situation in a clearer light. Diagrams can be used as guides to explore the overall structure of a problem and to reveal possible courses of action that might otherwise be missed. In some cases you may realize, upon studying your schematic, that your problem situation is too complicated to solve immediately.

You may then find it necessary to approach your problem, in steps and degrees, rather than in a single move.

Before going any further, let us not forget the extreme importance of identifying our final objective. If your objective is vague, too general, or even overly idealistic, you may never arrive at a satisfactory conclusion. Therefore, your goal must be realistic, sufficiently clear, and precise enough to serve as your basis upon which to proceed. Unless your situation has been well explored by you, choices are not likely to be obvious once your work begins. Thus your first move is to develop as clear a formulation of your objective as possible. You may even find it necessary to consult with one or more persons whom you consider qualified in your area of concern at this stage. But the question of your overall objective should never really be out of your mind.

It is interesting to note at this point that some secondary schools in Europe, as well as some elementary schools in the United States and England, emphasize problem-solving techniques as a regular part of their curriculum. This provides children with the skills and attitudes to locate, define, and analyze problems as found in school or in community life. Extracurricular activities, such as student clubs and student government, serve to reinforce problem-solving skills. This becomes an additional frame of reference to the students for understanding to some extent what is expected of them in later life. This makes them more fully equipped as future world citizens.

Those who are creatively endowed often decide that the best solution to the problem they have in mind, if it is of sufficient intensity and general interest, is to write a play, novel, or essay that exposes and brings to light in a realistic manner some actual social ill. Such themes as racism, anti-Semitism, female emancipation, greed, or corruption have all been dealt with extremely effectively by several writers. Protest songs or propaganda plays often stimulate thought and discussion on the part of the audience. These provide encouragement, which relieves, to some extent, the pressure of the problem which plagued the creator of the art form.

Regarding the use of intuitive insight on personal problems, we must first stress that you should have a clear understanding of the various principles or factors that bear on the problem and solution sought. You then actively consider what is required by the problem—that is to say, you note how its elements seem to be interrelated and seek some rule or guideline that might lead directly to the goal. Mental discipline and a willing flexibility should characterize your thinking as you guide yourself step by step according to your plan, and altering the plan itself, if need be, as you move toward a solution.

But there often comes a time when we are "stumped" for a solution. Even after the keenest and most penetrating consideration of a problem, we seem at a loss for an answer. At that point we should consider letting the problem go and handing it over to a Higher Judgment. In other words, we should release the entire issue to the subconscious mind for help and guidance. This is, admittedly, not an easy thing to do. Humans tend to want to *hold on* to problems and seek guidance from the reasoning mind only.

However, if we do successfully release our problem to our inner self, this greater guide within will at some time—be it hours, days, or weeks later—bring forcefully to our conscious mind an exalted judgment concerning our problem. The solution or method to proceed will seem completely right. We will entertain no doubts or hesitancy concerning the information given. In addition, there will be a kind of upliftment of our emotions or an excitement accompanying the message. The intuitive knowledge will either flash suddenly into the consciousness or slowly unfold in mind in progressive stages. This is the intelligence of the Cosmic Mind, which is resident within the inner subconscious arena. When this useful information enters our outer objective consciousness, it is commonly called a "hunch" or intuitive "feeling"—or to use current scientific terminology, which is just as accurate, "insight."

It must be emphasized here that the inner self will not aid us in the form of intuitive insight for problem solving unless we have first applied ourselves in some way, objectively, to solving our own problem. In other words, preliminary groundwork, as well as sincere effort and desire, must precede our handing over of the problem to the subconscious mind, for there to be the appropriate helpful insight. So, the more we know about our situation, the deeper we have penetrated and availed ourselves of problem-solving techniques as previously discussed, the more all-embracing we can expect our help to be from the Cosmic Mind, should we need it.

At any rate, the entire study of intuitive guidance is actually only one aspect of authentic mystical teachings. The overall nature of humanity—physical, mental, and spiritual—should be explored in great depth through years of study. The nature of the Cosmos, mental creating, development of psychic faculties, the strengthening of will, the elevation of character and personality, visualization, meditation, and many more categories, will aid in enriching the student's life as these types of teachings are meant to be put into practical application in daily life.

"Good advice may also be given silently, through our thoughts and actions in our daily lives."

Chapter 4

Giving Advice

The question is often asked: "I want to offer some mystical viewpoints to my friends in order to help them with various problems, but how do I effectively give advice?"

Let's first clear up one area of concern before moving into the realm of advising others. There seems to be a somewhat prevailing opinion among the general public that the Rosicrucian Order is some kind of secret organization, and that its members are prohibited from discussing it with nonmembers. Nothing could be further from the truth. As a matter of fact, students of AMORC may definitely discuss the Rosicrucian point of view with friends and family.

Students are encouraged to discuss at length, if they wish to do so, the concepts and principles they are taught. Serious students study the lessons, called "monographs." They contemplate the thoughts and ideas in these lessons, and they possibly attend a local affiliated group where they share ideas with friends. They are encouraged, furthermore, to apply the teachings in everyday life. Most of the topics that friends and acquaintances want to discuss concerning mysticism are not new to the average student. For instance, if someone mentions karma or reincarnation, or soul, the student is not lost. In all probability the student is able to talk for hours on any one of those subjects.

Basically, AMORC's membership guidelines state that non-members are not allowed to read the Order's private teachings. If a person is willing to commit him or herself to a serious study of mysticism and actually joins the organization, then that is a different story.

If one has studied for any length of time within the Rosicrucian system, that person will be surprised just how much has been slowly digested and made a part of one's own thought patterns as a result of judicious reflection upon these ideas, relevant experimentation, meditation, and practical application. The ability to see problems in a new or brighter light is being intensified. The unconditional love and concern for others is also greater. The desire to help others in some way becomes paramount. But how can a person help?

Ralph M. Lewis, the late president of the Rosicrucian Order, spoke in a lecture on a related subject. He referred to giving a precautionary warning to others. He suggested that if we know of an impending dangerous event, about which we have concrete or intuitive knowledge, and a friend will be directly involved, we should go ahead and inform that person as best we can under the circumstances.

We should let the person know that we are purely and simply attempting to be of service. We should not be overbearing or create the impression that we are alarmists. A sane and rational explanation of our feelings to that person will ". . . cause him to think. He may, however, take no heed and may disregard the whole incident as imaginary and ridiculous. But you have done your part."

In the above example, we referred more precisely to advising others, i.e., giving words of caution and warning. We mention this to differentiate between humanitarian admonishment, and the desire to give advice, to counsel, or to give instruction to our friends and family. Here is where we enter upon what has been called a touchy subject. Here is where our personal motives and qualifications for giving advice need to be examined very thoroughly. Moreover, did that person ask for help? Is he doing anything in his life to help himself? Does the student have courage and humility to refer the individual to another, more qualified person?

One school of thought says a person should *never* give advice, under any circumstances. That viewpoint may well be summed up by the American author Edward Newton, who said, "Only when a man is safely ensconced under six feet of earth with several tons of enlauding granite upon his chest, is he in a position to give advice with any certainty, and then he is silent."

We may be tempted to say that such a viewpoint is rather extreme and that its author may very well have gone overboard in his refusal to give advice. But if we put ourselves on the receiving end of incessant advice, we may be a bit more sympathetic with Mr. Newton. For instance, how often has a well-meaning person said to us, "If you want my advice, I would go right over there and tell that person a thing or two!" Have we actually taken that well-meaning advice? How about the people who are constantly giving you advice in the form of platitudes and bromides, such as, "a stitch in time saves nine," or "two heads are better than one," and on and on. Honestly, isn't it true that your psychological reaction at that time is to do just the opposite?

Unwanted or unsolicited advice will usually fall on deaf ears. Such advice is even more completely rejected if the person to whom we give the counsel notices that we are presently suffering under a similar condition. It is akin to an overweight person giving advice to another overweight person on how to diet. The admonishment, "Don't do as I do, do as I say," just doesn't work. People need a good example to go by. This brings us to another area of giving advice.

People who have overcome some test or trial in life or have obviously improved themselves in some manner are often looked up to for constructive guidance. For example, a person who has spent a great deal of time in trouble with the law and who subsequently turns his or her life completely around and becomes an outstanding citizen in the community is in an excellent position for giving advice to youthful offenders or recent parolees. In other words, that person has gone through the fire and knows exactly how to encourage and perhaps guide another person in similar circumstances. Of course, this help he or she may give hinges upon the fact that the young offender wants assistance.

Similarly, in talks about mystical subjects, speak authoritatively on the subject matter, or at least couch explanations as being one's best understanding of the subject. In other words, we would suggest that it would be a mistake to attempt a *personal* description of Nirvana while never having experienced it. Once again, make it clear that it is "our understanding" that such and such takes place in such a mental and spiritual condition. We may state in general how "our lessons refer to such a state of consciousness as being the main goal of the aspiring mystic," and so on. You may go on to explain how you personally hope to achieve such an exalted awareness through the lifetime to come, and so forth. But, once again, if such a condition of consciousness is not within your realm of individual experience, make certain that the listeners are crystal clear on this point. Such a description is purely explanatory in nature. Outside of that, such instruction is theoretical or, at best, intellectual speculation. It is best to admit a lack of knowledge than to attempt a fabrication. Others will respect your honesty.

The ancient Greek philosopher Thales demonstrated both wit and wisdom when asked what was difficult. He answered, "To know one's self." When asked what was easy, he replied, "To advise another."

This leads to still another pitfall to avoid. Ask yourself, "Why am I so desirous of going about giving advice to other people?" Be brutally frank. Pose the question to self, "Am I attempting to establish a reputation as a learned counselor?" "Am I looking for prestige, fame, admiration, love?" True, there is and must be a very real element of self-gratification, or better still, personal *enjoyment*, derived from the fact that we are able to help others to help themselves. But if conscience tells us that the predominant reason for giving advice is self-glorification, rest assured our pearls of wisdom will fall on deaf ears. Furthermore, there will most certainly be those listeners who will intuitively perceive our motives for what they really are. So try to avoid even the hint of self-exaltation.

Yet the question still remains: how best to give advice? Consider this scenario. A friend approaches and begins to talk to you about a problem. Naturally, you are sympathetic and attentive to that person. You will say that you are very sorry to learn of this situation and that you certainly hope things will work out to a satisfactory conclusion as time goes on. Remember, some persons simply need an understanding shoulder to lean on. They may not be seeking advice at all. Furthermore, they may not have given you the entire picture of the situation; therefore, your counsel will be incomplete. They just want to "get it off their chest," as the saying goes, and they may consider your advice as being uncalled for. You may say something similar to, "Is there anything I can do to help you?" But a word of caution is necessary: Be sure you are completely sincere when you ask, "Can I help?" A half-hearted gesture is certain to be recognized and refused. If the situation is one where there is no way to assist, then it is pointless to offer advice.

We suggest that since you will be in a relatively passive mood while the person is speaking, you make an unspoken suggestion to your inner self. Ask yourself, "Is there a way to help this person?" Once again, really mean it! As that person continues talking, chances are there may arise within your consciousness an avenue of thought, a plan of action, or a piece of advice to give to that person. How will you know that it is constructive advice coming from your greater self within? You will know by the fact that there will be no doubt in your objective mind at that moment as to the correctness of the instruction. Furthermore, your emotional nature will respond to the advice from within in an agreeable manner. In other words, you will somehow feel good about the plan or thought. It will seem clear and perfectly obvious to you that it is exactly what should be done or said. But the problem now is how to suggest this to the other person.

It is best if we can get that person to ask for advice before we give it. If an individual personally requests assistance, then that person has already placed himself or herself in a receptive frame of mind, and he or she may be more readily helped. Half the job is done. So, you might consider asking your friend with the problem, point blank, "Would you like me to suggest a way to help you?" A more roundabout way of doing it would be to state that you believe you know of a way to alleviate the situation. Say that if he or she doesn't mind, "an idea has just come to me that I believe will help you. May I tell you what it is?" In all likelihood, curiosity will prompt the person into listening to what you have to say. Present your idea to that person clearly and definitely.

Let us provide another word of caution: Just because the idea comes from your inner self is no reason to insist that the other person follow your advice. Say what you have to say and let it go at that. If the idea is cosmically inspired, then at least your good advice will be planted. The person may not immediately see the wisdom of your words, but perhaps eventually your friend will. But don't push, or you will lose all.

The primary goal of dedicated students of mysticism is self-improvement. That, in itself, is a never-ending task. Setting a good example enables us to help others in an unspoken way. Our way of thinking and doing things might well be noted by others and appreciated. In other words, good advice may also be given *silently*, through our thoughts and actions in our daily lives.

"The immutable cosmic forces are ever seeking a balance. The operation of this law of nature is absolutely and totally impersonal in its striving for harmony and balance."

Chapter 5

Karma

One of the most thought-provoking principles given within authentic mystical teachings is the concept of karma.

It is said that karma is the law of cause and effect. For every vibratory impulse of a positive or negative nature that we set into motion, it is asserted that there will be an equal reaction upon us, according to this law of nature. For example, for every bit of happiness and pleasure we give to others, we shall eventually receive a like amount of happiness and pleasure. On the other hand, for all the misery and suffering we cause, we will suffer in similar measure. It is further taught that the law of karma does not act in a revengeful manner, nor is it a concept of a human God giving humans a personal reward. Karma functions in order that we may learn lessons and thereby evolve our understanding of ourselves so that we may ultimately act more in harmony with universal laws. A little historical background concerning karma might be appropriate at this point.

Among the ancient Brahmans, a sect of the Hindu religion, we find that the doctrine of karma was widely accepted. They felt that the soul would achieve a happy or unhappy rebirth according to its works in a previous life. The gradual spread of mysticism among the Brahmans was thus encouraged, taking the form of a search for the ultimate personal union with God. It was believed that this, in turn, would produce a release from constant reincarnation and karma.

In ancient Egypt, an elaborate ritual of embalmment, known as mummification, was designed to save the corpse from decomposition and restore its faculties so that it could live in a well-equipped tomb. The idea was that on a future judgment day, the body would be resurrected and face the great god Osiris. The dead would then have to undergo a judgment on the moral and karmic quality of his or her past life on earth. In this ordeal, the deceased could be saved from an awful second death only by showing proof of personal integrity. If the test was safely passed, the dead would then be admitted into the heavenly realms over which Osiris ruled. The Osirian mortuary belief was practiced from about 2400 B.C. until its suppression during the Christian era. It is interesting to note that in some respects this belief constituted a forerunner, if not an actual prototype, of Christianity as a salvation religion.

Running through the great complex of doctrines and ritual practices of Hinduism was the belief in karma. The Hindus felt that the soul carried with it the burden of its past actions, and these past actions created the forms of its future incarnations. They felt that as long as the soul mistook the material world for true reality and clung to its material existence, it was doomed to suffer endless births and deaths. The release or "liberation" from this so-called misery consisted of the soul's full realization of its unity with the Supreme Essence. Some techniques used by the Hindus for this attainment consisted of mastering the meditative process, living the ascetic life, and an intense personal devotion to the deity.

The enlightenment attained by Gautama Buddha prompted him to expound on the cause of human existence in the material world—a world from which suffering inevitably arose. Buddhist teachings and practices, therefore, were designed to acquaint people with their true personal nature and enable them to free themselves from craving for existence in the time-space world. They would thus achieve *Nirvana*—the ultimate goal—a condition achieved when karma and the succession of lives and births had been overcome. To overcome one's karma, the disciple was expected to follow the Eightfold Path of Ethical Conduct. The eight paths were: right conduct, right thinking, right viewing, right aspiration, right effort, right speech, right livelihood, and right contemplation (or meditation).

It is interesting to note the parallel between the Christian religion and that of ancient Islam, in that both groups advocate the total submission of self to a deity in order to be relieved of karma, or sin. The saving power of Christ is fundamental to Christianity and finds expression in every aspect of its practice. The Islamic faith (inspired by Muhammad) states that submission to Allah is the means for overcoming trials in life.

According to Zoroastrianism of ancient Persia, good and evil forces struggled for mastery in the universe. Humans had to decide on which side to align themselves during a lifetime. Good was personified as the god Ormazd, and evil was named Ahriman. The karmic condition experienced as a happy or unhappy state was said to result from the decision made as to which concept to follow.

In the official Rosicrucian teachings the law of karma is that literally each act and even each thought must have and will have its resultant compensation. If we give a little thought to this straightforward way of viewing karma, we find that it is perhaps the most lucid way in the Western world to fully understand this law of nature.

To elaborate: the immutable cosmic forces are ever seeking a balance. This insistence on balance is reflected in events sometimes viewed by humanity as terrible and disastrous, as in the case of floods, earthquakes, and tornadoes. It is also personally felt by those who suffer the painful pang of conscience because of past thoughts and actions. The operation of this law of nature is absolutely and totally impersonal in its striving for harmony and balance.

Let me give you an example of an incorrect way of looking at karma. Let us say that there are two opposing weather patterns approaching each other in the atmosphere. The result might be a windstorm. In such a case we should not assign the inevitable outcome of these moving weather patterns as bad karma. It should not be considered good or evil, but is simply nature's way of achieving balance.

For further example, let's say that you are a person who enjoys competitive sports activities, such as gymnastics. You already know that there are many variables that go into the achievement of success, the prime one being yourself. If you are a consistently superior performer, or if you are a consistently poor performer, you may have had the tendency to say you were experiencing good karma or bad karma. However, the responsible, mystical way of viewing the situation is not that some deity above specially arranged for you to succeed or fail. Your skill as a result of *practice*, the condition of your health, your ability to *concentrate*, your perseverance, and many other factors, are all major contributing reasons for your dexterity in gymnastics. In a real sense, we might say we create our own karma.

That same impersonal judgment is present even in our workaday thoughts and contemplations. For instance, let's say in your place of employment there is a person who works near you. As the days and weeks pass by, for one reason or another, you almost unconsciously have allowed your mind to build up an intense dislike of this person. However, not wanting to produce an unpleasant atmosphere, you naturally do not voice this feeling, and you keep your opinion to yourself. But you allow yourself to secretly *burn* within, fanning the flames of your displeasure with imaginary scenarios of spite and negativity. On the surface, however, you are diplomatic and polite.

Serious students of mysticism know that others, if they have any degree of psychic awareness or psychic sensitivity, will eventually realize our true feelings. Therefore, this other individual eventually comes to know how you truly feel about him, and he, in turn, begins to react the same way toward you. You then begin to become aware of his hostility.

In such a case, we most certainly would not be justified in exclaiming: "Why do I have such bad karma as to work in this stressful environment?" In this particular case, we are the *prime movers*. Our own thoughts and ideas radiating from us dictate on an impersonal basis, through the law of cause and effect, what we will eventually experience. Remember the basic premise that each action and even each thought will produce a karmic effect.

Moreover, we will come to this painful realization of the negative thoughts of our co-worker when we will be most keenly aware of the *lesson* to be learned. In other words, experiences of karmic reactions will not be superficial wounds; they will cut deep. They will make us think. They tend toward making us examine not the other person, but ourselves. We then typically begin to seek ways and means to change our future thoughts and actions to higher and nobler considerations than in the past. This deeply searching experience thereby helps us to evolve ourselves just a bit more and balance the scales of justice.

Looking briefly at another way of dealing with karma as practical mysticism, let's say you find yourself in an environment where hatred, jealousy, and other types of negative feelings are *already* present. Refuse to allow other persons to control your thoughts. You should attempt to be the master of your self. You most certainly would not wish to add to the negative conditions around you by joining in the prevailing poisonous atmosphere.

We suggest that each and every day that you are temporarily in such a place, you consciously attempt to raise your thoughts to a higher level. Persistently seek the good in others around you, and make every attempt to mentally understand the true nature of the problems surrounding you. We realize that this is a difficult task, one that will call upon your utmost efforts at self-discipline and attunement with Cosmic Mind. But once you begin achieving the light of knowledge and an understanding of the root cause of problems that confront you, the darkness of jealousy and hatred will seem to burn away as does the morning fog before the rising sun.

There is another side to the above example that also has to do with karma and practical mysticism: For each attempt on your part to understand your condition, for every effort you make to rise above your situation, and because of the feelings of unconditional love and kindness you have exhibited, you are building up for yourself a beneficial karmic condition that will eventually be balanced. In other words, you have stored up for yourself a credit to your account.

Jesus the Christ called it "riches in heaven," or good karma. There is an overbalance in your favor and the Cosmic Intelligence will restore that balance, perhaps not immediately, but at a time when you will need it most. Once again we note an impersonal act of nature operating through a completely understandable law—namely, the law of cause and effect, or karma.

We have discussed karma in the light of both a historical perspective and our inner thoughts and contemplations. But what about overt physical acts? Is it not obviously true that some persons are conscientiously striving for the better things of life, doing good deeds for others, and not really reaping the good effects of karma? On the other hand, how about the apparently negative cases, those we know of who seem to avoid responsibilities? They sometimes go to their graves apparently free and clear. What about those people?

The basic premise is this: the law of karma is neither rewarding us for good deeds nor punishing us for bad deeds. The balancing out of the scale of justice, the harmonizing action on the part of the Cosmic, will take place perhaps in another lifetime, when all conditions are correct for a learning experience to take place in consciousness. The fact that a person (now living happily or suffering miserably) does not remember a past life reveals the fact that Cosmic Mind brings lessons to our consciousness and is not personally chastising us like a taskmaster or merely giving us gifts like Santa Claus.

If we decide that we are in a distressing condition, we should immediately begin instituting the opposite vibratory impulse. We seek understanding and a way to change ourselves for the better, regardless of the fact that the cause of our suffering may have been instituted in another life. If we are happy, we seek to share this with others and steadfastly maintain or even expand these joyful conditions.

An excellent overall goal would be to eliminate as much negative karma for ourselves as we can during this present lifetime and, at the same time, to put the cosmic forces in our debt with beneficial karma to as great a degree as humanly possible.

"We exist in the eternal now. The future constantly converts itself into now, then instantly becomes the past, like a stream rushing down a mountainside."

Chapter 6

The Next Ten Years

A student once made this remark, "Ten years ago, while riding in public transportation in a large American city, I received a psychological shock that jarred me out of my normal lethargy. The impact came from, of all things, a public service poster. The announcement showed a picture of a grim, sweaty man, carrying a massive load of bricks. The caption read something like this: 'You won't get tomorrow's jobs with yesterday's skills.' I suddenly saw myself as being the laborer in that advertisement and realized I had fallen into a state of inertia in life. Stunned and dazed, I began to mobilize my inner forces toward advancement on all levels."

Perhaps the depth of the internal collision, experienced by this student who corresponded with us, can be gauged by the fact that he didn't simply say, "Oh, I have to get a better job." Although that would have been commendable, he realized instead that real preparation for the future should be taken on *all* levels: physical, mental, and spiritual.

Of course, personal advancement can mean different things to different people. One student recalled being seated at her desk during a break period in a large and busy government office, reading an issue of the *Rosicrucian Digest*, a magazine featuring mysticism, science, and the arts. A co-worker approached her and asked, "What is that you're reading?" Our correspondent, being a careful and intuitive person, desirous of giving an encouraging response, fixed her eyes on the man in front of her, but immediately experienced a feeling of aversion. Thus repelled, she replied simply: "It has to do with self-improvement." Her fellow-worker laughed derisively and said, "Give me a million dollars, and I'll be self-improved."

As trite as his reply was, he did live up to his personal creed in life to the utmost, according to his inner development. Several months later he was reportedly under indictment by federal authorities for taking bribes while in office.

When tackling large-scale revisions in life, it is possible to go so far as to even contemplate your next incarnation—if reincarnation is something you believe in. But we suggest you start small and work up. Try this scenario: look ahead—say a decade from now. What do you see yourself doing then? Have you elevated your mind and character to a higher level? Are you a calmer, more wholesome and decent person, one whom others love to be near? Have you discarded shopworn and tawdry ideals for the more noble and beautiful things of life?

It is important to be aware of the trend of the times, to prepare oneself for adequate future employment or happier times of relaxation in retirement. Above that in importance, however, is the search for personal fulfillment, the fitting into society in accordance with one's own personality. After all, we are each a unique being, and every one of us has his or her own divinity within available for guidance and inspiration in life. Not everyone can or should be pursuing the electronics field. Nor should everyone attempt to be an opera singer. In looking ahead, toward the next ten years, different persons hold different hopes and dreams, depending on their age and a variety of other factors.

As stated above, persons in their middle years might tend to see themselves as being retired ten years from now. What does one do all day long when retired? Persons much younger may desire to be accomplished professionals, regularly employed in this or that endeavor. How does one go about getting from here to there? *Now* is the time to ask these questions, not ten years from now.

Let's look at our life-scenario from a slightly different angle for a moment. What about ten years *ago*? What were you doing? Perhaps a better question is why were you doing it? Did the people, objects, plans, and ideals you pursued then result in an improved condition for yourself today? What could have been done better? What did you do right? Where did you go wrong?

In viewing the past, we do not advocate over-indulgence in remorse and bitter regret. After all, life can hold sufficient sorrows without us arbitrarily manufacturing even more. It is healthy to have a penitent attitude over lost opportunities, but we also advocate that one mentally move ahead to the present and plan for the future. It is well to learn from the past, but decidedly unhealthy to constantly live in it.

So, in looking back, we focus on the positive, instructional aspects of our past deeds and attitudes. But how about the present? Can we now hope for a better tomorrow? Should we dream of a glorious day to come? Do we sit about and wish for a better life? While it is preferable to keep the sunshine in our lives rather than anxiously anticipate doom and disaster, it is even better to plan for the future consciously and realistically.

The past is in memory and nothing can change it; the future is our potential in imagination and visualization; but the present is all we can really experience. We exist in the *eternal now*. The future constantly converts itself into now, then instantly becomes the past, like a stream rushing down a mountainside.

To briefly summarize, the past is ever a memory. We should deemphasize regrets and use what we have learned to help us in our daily lives. The present is best served not so much by idle dreaming, but by formulating a practical design for the future.

As stated, when we view the future, we use the mental faculty called *imagination*. Better still is the mystical technique of drawing upon cosmic forces and mentally pinpointing a specific goal to be accomplished. After this is done, this ideal goal should be released from further mental concern. Then, step by step, our goal may be brought into fruition, with inner cosmic guidance and help.

With this visualization technique, mystical students not only marshal their thoughts and organize them into a coherent and unified whole, but they submit this plan, this finished picture, to the higher judgment and wisdom of God within. We'll have much more to say about visualization a little later on.

Meanwhile, though it is good to work for, plan, and visualize well into the future so as to achieve much better tomorrows, it is just as important to remain in daily attunement. Living each and every day to its fullest potential can make one's entire lifetime a wonderful journey.

"What do we suggest to ourselves on a daily basis? Is it hatred, fear, doubt, illness, discord, and failure; or love, courage, health, harmony, and success?"

Chapter 7

What Do You Suggest?

Before considering the subject of visualization, let's discuss an often-overlooked aspect of mystical work called *suggestion*. To begin with, what are some of the definitions of suggestion? How and when do we go about utilizing these in order to help ourselves? And, what are the time-honored principles involved in this process that we should be aware of at this time?

Let's first consider what may be termed a negative implication of suggestion. Suggestion, of course, is the process by which one thought leads to another, especially through the association of ideas. For instance, one's fear of the dark is usually entirely due to self-suggestion. Another example is a person allergic to roses who develops an asthma attack when looking through a seed catalogue. Expanding upon this line of thought, there is what is termed *subliminal stimulation,* or the presentation of some stimuli from an outside source to our consciousness that is either too brief or too faint, or both, for us to be fully conscious of its impression upon us.

This rather interesting form of indirect suggestion has been discussed in the past in the form of television commercials or commercials in movie theaters. In the latter case, popcorn or perhaps soda pop would be flashed onto the movie screen and then be quickly removed before the viewer entirely realized it on a conscious level. But, the theory affirms, one's inner self would receive the message, and the viewer then would begin to feel hungry or thirsty.

In the Shakespearean play *Othello*, the villain, Iago, systematically drops subtle hints and indirect suggestions regarding Othello's wife, Desdemona, and her possible infidelity. The poisonous suggestions are slowly compounded through the play until the protagonist, Othello, in a final jealous rage, murders his innocent wife.

This indirect suggestion is also utilized in the form of what is termed "prestige suggestion." This is where a famous person claims to use an advertised product, and we, are thus being told in a subtle way that it is "safe" or "best" to follow that advice. This form of suggestion of a prestige or social nature branches out into recommendations from these famous people concerning widely differing areas of interest. For instance, we may be subtly told that a particular insurance plan is a good one, because Mr. X, who is a well-known actor, says so. This type of suggestion also extends into the common practice we see whereby an interviewer will very seriously solicit the views of a popular entertainer soliciting his or her opinion about how the United Nations should function—in spite of the fact that this prominent person may have no experience whatsoever in world government or even local politics. It is purely and simply a case of prestige suggestion being presented to the viewing public. The mystical aspects of the misuse of suggestion will be discussed a little later on.

In this discussion, we are chiefly concerned with *autosuggestion*—the suggestions we give to ourselves. A concise definition of autosuggestion is: "a subtle command of one's objective mind to the subconscious mind." Through the use of will power, we mentally focus our attention upon a specific desire and then transfer it to our deeper self for operation. It is best to realize that when the outer, objective consciousness is at rest, the inner subconscious is susceptible to suggestion. Let's explore this interesting concept a little more.

We know that we are subject to the influx of energy from the great Cosmic Mind. This energy is inexhaustible. We have the ability, should we choose to use it, to concentrate this energy within ourselves in order to bring about beneficial results. The beneficial influence of the mind upon an improper condition, or illness of the body, is in all likelihood familiar to each of you. This influence lies solely in the focus and direction of it by us. For example, when we were children, we took a small magnifying glass outdoors on a sunny day and focused the sun's energy through the glass onto a piece of paper. The tiny pinpoint of concentrated sunlight eventually heated up the paper to such a degree that the paper burst into flames.

Therefore, we now symbolically recognize the sun as being the ever-present energy of the Cosmos, the magnifying glass as our focused mind power, and the flaming paper as the direct result of our concentrated effort.

To reemphasize, we should definitely be aware that we can also *unconsciously* transmit this force of energy within us. This is known by the advertising industry, as mentioned earlier, and we are bombarded by cleverly worded statements suggesting that we "may" be suffering from one ailment or another because of a variety of symptoms. We then begin feeling ill. Then it is suggested that if we purchase this or that remedy, we will feel better.

The remedies are of endless variety: some of them are good, some are ridiculous, and some have even proven to be fraudulent. But the interesting fact is that in some viewers' experience, the remedy or even a placebo, actually worked! Again, the unconscious suggestion to self produced an unshakeable faith in the product, thereby changing the direction of this same force of internal energy from a negative suggestion of illness to a positive one of emerging health.

When would be the best time to employ important suggestions to self? It has been found that the early morning hours are best for memory work. Memorizing, of course, is nothing more than a series of suggestions forcefully directed to the subconscious mind. Naturally, the mental activity should be conducted before breakfast, while the body is not actively engaged in digesting food and other fundamental activities. Also, at this time we are fresh, our brain is not cluttered with problems of the day, and we are not physically fatigued. For those who might be having difficulty memorizing certain passages that must be remembered, try the early morning hours, before breakfast.

Passing on to the deeper and even more serious aspects of autosuggestion, some people may be plagued by a mental fixation, some form of fear, for example. This fear often results in such agonizing manifestations as stammering or acute stage fright, or some serious intestinal disorders, for example. Self-analysis on the part of the individual student is called for in these important cases to discover the root of a particular problem. It is best to be absolutely and totally honest with yourself as you probe more deeply within to discover the truth. Once the mind is reasonably clear as to what the problem is, put self-suggestion to work in the following manner.

In the first place, personal problems, such as fear, are best dealt with at night upon retiring to bed, not in the morning, as in the case of memory work. Naturally, the body will be tired, the mind will tend to replay the day's events, and the tendency to worry over them may also be present. If none of these annoying conditions are present, all the better. If they are, it is best to exercise control over self and prepare for sleep. Willfully cast out all other thoughts and concentrate the whole attention on the problem at hand. What is to be envisioned as a suggestion? For instance, if the problem is the inability to break a habit, such as smoking, hold a crystal clear mental picture of yourself while absolutely and totally rejecting a cigarette the next morning.

Suggestion to self the night before must in truth be more of a definite command to the inner self. It cannot be vague or abstract. It is in fact a decree to the subconscious mind. The wording of the command must be concentrated or reduced to its bare essentials. While picturing the action taking place, proclaim to the inner self, "Tomorrow, I will do this." Then go to sleep.

If it is a constructive thought, the subconscious mind will immediately accept it, and it will be the beginning of a self-established *law*. This law is another word for a habit—a counter-habit that has been willfully established deep within. This suggestion to self should be reinforced nightly until the habit is as firmly entrenched, or even more so, than the original condition. Evenings, mornings, and even a quiet period during the day can be used for this extremely important mystical activity. This is just one aspect of practical mysticism that sincere students can put into regular application.

Again, we must emphasize one more point here before concluding this chapter, and that is the attempted misuse of suggestion. To explain briefly, if one's suggestion is constructive, the inner mind will readily accept it. Therefore, autosuggestions, or subtle commands to the subconscious mind, should be of a nature that does not interfere with the constructive principle of the Cosmic Mind within. In other words, this sacred force within is always attempting to help us, to further our progress on all beneficial levels. Should we submit something diametrically opposed to this constructive energy, it will be sent back to the objective level of consciousness, and we will be expected to reason through our plan before again submitting it. It is interesting to note, however, that we can in fact eventually establish a negative habit within ourselves, but it has been found to take a great many repetitions before it becomes effective. It is *much* easier to establish constructive ideals because they are in harmony with our inner self and we will truly be working along the lines of least resistance.

And so, the question must be asked: What do we suggest to ourselves on a daily basis? Is it habitually hatred, fear, doubt, illness, discord, and failure? Or do we suggest love, courage, health, harmony, and success?

It was Buddha who said, "Let the wise man guard his thoughts, for they are difficult to perceive, very artful, and they rush wherever they list. Thoughts well guarded bring happiness."

"If men and women are
to achieve a satisfactory life,
they need to keep contact
with the earth and to cultivate
their imaginations."

Chapter 8

What Is Visualization?

What is visualization and how does one visualize? The answer to this inquiry often lies in knowing what true visualization is *not*, and then in practicing special exercises, as given in authentic mystical teachings, in order to arrive at a clear personal interpretation of what visualization is.

Let's establish at the outset of this discussion that visualization, like intuition, must be worked at. Once you have a good idea of what you are trying to accomplish, the rest of it takes patience and effort. In other words, development of the psychic faculties, one of which is the use of visualization, will not be automatically apparent, just because you intellectually comprehend the subject matter. Inner self-development is very much like the planting of a seed. Even with the most loving care, you will not see a tree tomorrow, next week, or next month. But in time, the seed will germinate and psychic development will take firm root within you. The fruit thereof will be for your benefit and the benefit of others. But, again, it takes time.

Visualization is not hallucination. Hallucination is the perception of objects with no actuality. It is an experience of sensations with no external cause and usually arises from disorders or actual diseases of the nervous system. This completely unfounded or mistaken impression can also be produced by the use of hallucinogenic drugs, such as mescaline. Alcohol abuse is also known to produce hallucinations, called *delirium tremens*, or D.T.'s. Hallucinations normally produce a fearful state of mind, if not actual terror and panic. It goes without saying that medical help is most definitely called for in cases of those persons subject to hallucinations.

Visualization is not an illusion. An illusion is a misconception of actuality or a perception that fails to give the true character of an object. Misleading visual images include optical illusions. Heat rays shimmering on the road ahead produce the illusion of pools of water. We are all aware of the common illusion of railroad tracks appearing to meet in the distance, usually at the horizon. Sherwood Anderson pointed out a more serious illusion many of us harbor when he commented, "Most modern great men are mere illusions sprung out of a national hunger for greatness."

Illusions, however, may be used for our benefit, as when we "open up" and improve the ambience of a small, dark room through the artful use of brighter lighting and a well-placed mirror, giving the illusion of spaciousness. Therefore, illusions can be useful as well as detrimental, as long as we have a firm grasp on the differences between truth and deception. The illusions of the five physical senses are discussed to some degree at various points in the Rosicrucian teachings.

As we approach visualization more closely, a little summing up at this point may be beneficial. Illusions and hallucinations are our perceptual experiences that seem to contradict objective actuality. In an illusion, we misinterpret sensory stimuli as in a person "supposing a bush to be a bear," to quote Shakespeare. By contrast, hallucinations appear to arise when there is no external source of stimulation, as when one flees an imaginary wolf or has bizarre hallucinatory dreams brought on by a high fever.

Visualization is not imagination. Imagination is creating things mentally by bringing together unrelated elements and building them into something concrete and definite in your mind. As a mystical student, one's imagination should be creative and progressive, and not engaged in mere fantasizing and daydreaming. Authors employ fertile imaginations in order to produce acceptable plots for their novels or short stories. Painters utilize imagination in bringing together oft-unrelated elements so as to bind together a cohesive and beautiful work of art. Continuing the theme of the positive use of imagination, H.G. Wells stated that all youth spend much time in fanciful reveries, but the youths with "stronger minds anticipate and rehearse themselves for life in a thousand imaginations." The poet Samuel Coleridge also felt that imagination was the superior power over mere daydreaming fancy. He said, "Imagination is the higher faculty, the power that synthesizes raw experience into concrete images, and that fused contrary elements of feeling, vision, and thought into a unified whole."

The novelist and critic E.M. Forster attempted to point out the need for humanity to be aware of and work with the two worlds of materialism and idealistic imagination. He suggested that the cultivation of either in isolation is not enough. He felt that reliance on the earth alone often leads to a sort of callousness, whereas *exaggerated* development of imagination may tend to undermine the individual's sense of reality. Forster stated, "If men and women are to achieve a satisfactory life, they need to keep contact with the earth *and* to cultivate their imaginations."

Visualization is therefore neither hallucinations nor illusions, nor is it strictly imagination. Imagination is, however, an important first step toward the visualization process.

Visualization is a mental picture that you depict on the screen of your consciousness. You do not hallucinate; you do not fool yourself with an illusion; you do not bring together unrelated elements to produce an acceptable whole cloth, although, as stated, imagination is a preliminary step. In other words, you must first imagine an image.

The most effective employment of visualization entails not simply the depicting of a specific scene in our consciousness but includes also the releasing, the *letting go*, of this impression from the mind for a specific reason. Let's examine this in detail.

The most forceful way to concentrate upon a subject is to visualize it, to translate it into the form of a clear picture. There is nothing that the mind can think of that cannot be visualized or imaged. Backtracking briefly, there is a difference between imaging and imagining. You may imagine many wonderful things as they pour through your stream of consciousness and still not *image* what you are considering. To visualize is to image! It means creating in the mind's eye a picture that is filled with all of the details and parts connected with some thought, idea, or problem.

When you are building thought pictures in this way for the purpose of bringing about some definite result, keep in mind the fact that the picture you build should consist of the *final scene* of the thing you wish accomplished. If it is the desire to have someone send you an e-mail message, then your thought picture should be of your receiving a message from that person. If the desire concerns someone buying a piece of property from you, then the thought picture should be of a prospective customer concluding the sale with you. If the picture involves the starting of a plan, the picture you build in your mind should be the *crucial* point in the transaction where your culminating act is to be performed. By holding such a picture in your mind, you make it potentially a creative thought form.

To visualize masterfully means that you are able to close your eyes, anywhere, at any time, and willfully see in the mind's eye a picture of the condition you wish to create. You must, however, see it clearly, distinctly, as a living thing, in all its details and just the way you want it to be. This requires a strong ability to concentrate. You must lose your inner consciousness of where you are, who you are, and shut out all distractions.

A good exercise to begin this process would be to carefully observe a room in your home. First, notice the details in the colors of the furniture, the pictures on the walls, and so on. Then go to another room, close your eyes, and put together into a mental picture all the details, one by one, that you noted in the room you just left. In another application of this same principle, you might consider studying someone's face, or a good photograph of a scene or person. Then close your eyes and recreate that face or scene in your mind's eye. Do it until you are satisfied with the results. This technique is a slow process but a necessary one if you wish to have a perfectly visualized picture.

It should be interjected at this point that some mystical students are sight-impaired. Therefore, discussions of seeing and visualizing might appear to exclude them. However, this is not the case at all. When the ability to see clearly is not present, it is suggested that the student utilize one or more of the other four senses to mentally create their clear "picture." The picture might therefore include the sense of smell, taste, touch, or hearing. Any and all of these senses should certainly be added to the image being created.

Let's try a little experiment with consciousness. For the next few seconds, sit relaxed and silently decide which is the primary project, condition, situation, or problem facing you in your life at present. After you have decided upon a specific problem to work with, choose a harmonious final outcome of your problem. Take all the time you need to do this.

Next, concentrate your mind upon the final, clear solution in picture or image form that you wish to *release* into the greater Cosmic Consciousness. Slowly create the details of the picture. Carefully observe your image to see if there are any critical factors being left out. Your mind should be totally engrossed in the picture. Be assured that while this is occurring, the picture is being slowly and carefully attuned with the Cosmic.

When this important phase of your mental work is complete, you will then visualize the entire scene in your mind clearly and distinctly. This final state should last only a few seconds. Then you should take a deep breath and hold it for a few seconds, all the while holding the perfected thought in mind. As you exhale slowly, say to yourself words to this effect: "Into the Cosmic, I now release this impression. So be it."

Now comes the most important part of this entire process—and for some mystical students the most difficult. After your statement, "So be it," dismiss the picture from your mind. Give it no further thought. This may be done by conducting the exercise just before going to sleep at night. Or you may busily engage yourself in some other activity, such as turning on the radio or reading an interesting book. Whatever you do, it is most important that you stop the objective thinking process with respect to your image. If you allow the picture to remain in your mind, you keep it from being released into the Cosmic. It would be like a person who carefully writes an important letter, seals it in an envelope, stamps it, and then puts the letter in her pocket rather than mailing it.

So now we are beginning to realize the importance of correctly understanding what visualization is and how to visualize. This mystical tool will serve us well throughout this lifetime if we put it into practical use. Knowledge without application remains in the realm of mere intellectual speculation.

Sir Francis Bacon summed it up quite neatly when he said, "Chiefly, the mold of a man's fortune is in his own hands."

"Students of mysticism must be willing to face themselves on their own; they must fearlessly set aside outworn principles and thought patterns and be willing to examine a different approach to life and its complexities.

This cannot be done for you."

Chapter 9

Your Desire to Know

By reading this book, you are expressing your desire to know more about practical mysticism. You are tacitly admitting that there are areas in life about which you are not completely informed. You seek further light in your life. Such an attitude of humility and searching is a major step toward learning.

Allow us to establish at the outset of this discussion that the status or condition you find yourself in at present, with respect to your business, domestic, or philosophical beliefs, is the result of what you have created over the past months and years of your life. By seeking more knowledge about mysticism as a way of life, you are also seeking a practical and livable philosophy, one that will help and guide you through life's many problems and obstacles. However, let's establish another point at the outset: although mysticism offers a pragmatic way of dealing with our personal situation in life through physical and metaphysical principles, students of mysticism must be willing to face themselves on their own; they must fearlessly set aside outworn principles and thought patterns and be willing to examine a different approach to life and its complexities. This cannot be done for you.

The Rosicrucian Order in particular states that you, the sincere student, will be able to create for yourself the opportunities for greater inner unfoldment. You will not wait for an accident to happen or wish that things were better. You will systematically carve out your own niche in life. We know that opportunities present themselves *throughout* life, and that we ourselves formulate the conditions by which we may establish the kind of life that makes us happy.

We have all said of others who seem so successful in a particular field of endeavor, "what a lucky person," or "she's got it made," or "he's got it really good in life." Setting aside the obvious fact that every person on earth has problems, regardless of how comfortable he or she may appear, we realize that most of these people we envy have spent years in quietly creating their own environment. There are the classic examples of famous actors and actresses who many people constantly say were "overnight successes." If you closely examine their beginnings, you will probably discover the bitter struggles they had to endure; the hardships, mental and physical; the many years of preparation and frustration before even the smallest avenue for advancement was opened to them. This is true with many professions.

The question must now be asked: Are you willing to figuratively take *your personality* in hand and submit it to the same type of slow discipline and refinement?

Make no mistake about it; it takes a very special kind of courage to admit ignorance and submit to self-reformation. In fact, it takes a lot more inner discipline to refine and perfect ourselves than it takes to find a better job. As stated before, your admission of your willingness to learn is a major step in the right direction.

One aspect of this process of learning and inner growth arising in some of your minds is that you may feel age is a condition that will hinder you. Again, allow me to state emphatically that whether you consider yourself too young or too old is a *self-created obstacle* that will effectively block your possible growth just as surely as if you put a brick wall in front of you. Let us examine the first case in point.

For example, you may say, "I'm too young to tie myself down to one philosophy. I want to experiment for several years and perhaps, later in life, settle on a way to live." To this we state that you may visit a public library or perhaps a metaphysical bookstore, obtain each and every book on the shelf that pertains to some area of mysticism, read each publication, then visit numerous mystical groups, and superficially examine a great many philosophies for a great many years. At the end of that time, you will have gained a confusing cross section of viewpoints, be knowledgeable in not one single area and, more importantly, have derived only a minimum of inner self-development. In truth, you may have voluntarily missed valuable years in which you could have been dramatically discovering and unfolding yourself. We know for a fact that many have done exactly what I have just outlined, and they have reported that after having affiliated with a substantial organization, they sincerely regret not having begun their real studies years before. What are the general contents of such studies? We shall briefly discuss this a little later.

What about those who consider themselves too old to learn? With regard to learning what true mysticism has to offer students, we definitely state that no matter what your age, if you can read and understand what you read, you can still lift yourself up out of whatever rut you think you are now in. You may begin your mystical studies with the faith and confidence that you will gain a clearer insight into yourself and the world around you, regardless of your age and prevailing conditions. In fact, we can state without fear of contradiction that the truly sincere student is never too old to learn.

We say that people are never too old to learn as long as they do not arbitrarily establish a relationship between advanced age and the ability to learn. In other words, if you have decided that after a certain age you will no longer be able to absorb new information, then you have consciously conditioned yourself to come to a halt at that age. Actually, as we advance in age, although the desire for physical acquisitions diminishes, the desire for esthetic growth, for psychic unfoldment, quickens. There appears to be a proportionate lowering of physical drives and a concomitant rising of psychic goals.

As we grow older, we tend to become interested in the finer things in life, such as visiting museums or attending art lectures and musical concerts. We also tend to search deeper inside ourselves for answers to the many religious and philosophical questions in life. As a general rule, these questions are not always answered for us in life while we are engaged in making as much money as possible. While I do not negate the importance of living a comfortable life, what I am saying is that the truly important questions we all ask ourselves tend to remain unanswered regardless of our income, business status, social condition, or how much physical property we own.

It is interesting to note that, as a general rule, the faculty of imagination does not diminish with age. The young person with an active imagination continues to retain this quality in later life. This faculty will aid you in your mystical studies. Some examples of those who either began learning or continued growing at an advanced age are as follows.

Cato, the Roman philosopher, began to study the Greek language at the age of 80; Socrates, at an advanced age, learned to play musical instruments; Plutarch, when between 70 and 80 years of age, began to learn Latin; Rameau did not write a single opera until he was in his 50s. At age 54, he wrote *Castor et Pollux*, which was a great success, as were most of his later works composed during the following twenty-three years. The composer Verdi produced his greatest operas, *Aida* and *Othello*, after his 60th year. *Falstaff,* his last and arguably his greatest work, was not written until he was 80 years old. Critics noted that he showed not only "an unimpaired, but a progressive and novel style." We note the great cellist Pablo Casals was active until passing through transition at the age of 97. Ogilby, the translator of Homer and Virgil, was completely unacquainted with Greek or Latin until he was past 50. Benjamin Franklin did not begin his philosophical studies until he was over 50, and he is now best remembered as a writer, inventor, and philosopher.

History is filled with excellent examples of those who continued to contribute to the good of humanity well into maturity. Here are just a few others for your contemplation: Nelson Mandela was inaugurated as President of South Africa at the age of 75; Helen Keller published the book *Teacher,* honoring miracle worker Anne Sullivan, at the age of 75; Pablo Picasso painted his famous *Rape of the Sabines* at 81; Dame Agatha Christie, at age 84, oversaw production of the film version of her novel *Murder on the Orient Express*; Golda Meir served as Prime Minister of Israel from age 70 through 76; I.M. Pei designed the

Rock and Roll Hall of Fame in Cleveland, Ohio, at the age of 78; Alfred Hitchcock continued directing great suspense movies into his mid-70s; Michelangelo continued designing and creating until his death at the age of 88; Antonio Stradivari fashioned two of his most famous violins, the *Habeneck* and the *Muntz,* in his early 90s.

Other well-known personalities who continued working and creating good for humanity into their golden years include: Siddhartha Gautama, Galileo, George Frederick Handel, Immanuel Kant, Noah Webster, Ray Charles, Dr. Seuss, Toni Morrison, Winston Churchill, Eleanor Roosevelt, Leonard Bernstein, Arthur Rubinstein, Harriet Tubman, Laurence Olivier, Frederick Douglass, Katherine Hepburn, and Mother Teresa. The list, of course, goes on and on.

At this point it might be well to state clearly and concisely exactly what the Rosicrucian Order, AMORC, is. "The Rosicrucian Order is a philosophical and initiatic tradition. As students progress in their studies, they are initiated into the next level or degree. Rosicrucians are men and women around the world who study the laws of nature in order to live in harmony with them. Individuals study the Rosicrucian lessons in the privacy of their own homes on subjects such as the nature of the soul, developing intuition, classical Greek philosophy, energy centers in the body, and self-healing techniques. The

Rosicrucian tradition encourages each student to discover the wisdom, compassion, strength, and peace that already reside within each of us."

The teachings of the Rosicrucian Order are not for sale; they are given free to its students. There is a system of dues payments that takes care solely of such important considerations as the administrative functions, postage, local taxes, etc. The general operating costs are met on an equal basis by all members by means of the aforementioned dues. There are no other costs or obligations imposed.

As promised, here are some of the subjects discussed within the framework of the actual Rosicrucian lessons: karma; visualization; time and space; the relationship between body, mind and soul; concentration; meditation; reincarnation; life's cycles; the four principal manifestations of matter; psychic body; intuition; and a great many other topics are thoroughly covered step by step. The list is indeed quite lengthy. The studies progress for a number of years. In addition, there are many exercises and experiments given in the lessons to aid in personal understanding and mystical development.

The Rosicrucian system trains the mind, develops latent talent, and awakens interest in various fields of endeavor all geared toward self-improvement on all levels. Is there ever a time when any of us will know too much about these things? It is not too early to begin learning, and it most certainly is not too late!

Without the desire to learn, one is no longer fully alive as a human being, for to stop learning is to be partially dead. Through the acquisition of knowledge and the intelligent, humane application of that knowledge, one approaches a display of divine supremacy on earth.

"We reach deep within ourselves
for contact with that anchor,
that stronghold, where peace
and harmony reign supreme
at all times."

Chapter 10

Are You a Human Barometer?

"How should we, as students of mysticism, cope with life's pressures and anxieties? A promotional leaflet that was disseminated at one time by the Rosicrucian Order asked in its headline an interesting and provocative question: "Are You a Human Barometer?" It went on to question whether one's sense of balance and equilibrium was dependent upon every shift of the wind or turn of the tide. Furthermore, it encouraged one to seek a stabilizing influence in life through sensible and rational mystical studies.

A barometer, of course, is a device that measures atmospheric pressure. The most common type utilizes a column of mercury that coincides with the prevailing atmospheric pressure. The liquid mercury rises and falls a small amount in accordance with the variations of the weight of a column of atmosphere. Another type, the aneroid barometer, measures atmospheric pressure without the use of liquid. This barometer has an indicating needle or pointer mechanically attached to it. As this capsule-styled barometer with flexible walls changes in accordance with atmospheric pressure, the spring action needle indicates such fluctuations on a graph.

In the animal kingdom, certain species are reported to exhibit nervousness and fear before an earthquake or a tsunami strikes. A shift in atmospheric pressure is suspected as being the cause of this behavior. And there dwells in the Great Barrier Reef off the northeast coast of Australia the *barometer crab*, a lilac-colored creature whose deep red spots vary in accordance with changes in the weather.

The leaflet I mentioned earlier, however, did not question the operation of the mechanical indicators, nor did it explore the reactions of animals under pressure. Instead it asked quite forcefully, "Are you a *human* barometer?"

Mechanical devices are designed to be of service to humanity. They assist not only the meteorologist in weather forecasting, but also aid in a wide-ranging field of atmospheric sciences. They are inorganic substances made from the crust of the earth. Animal reactions are the result of organic creatures adjusting involuntarily to their environment and its pressures at any given time. As a result, they exhibit pleasure, pain, irritation, and so on. They do not, however, have a choice of reaction.

We, as humans, for the most part do have a choice of reaction to our environment and its pressures. Whether or not we decide to exercise that freedom of choice is one subtle but distinct difference between the behavior of animals and the behavior of the more evolved species of living things called *Homo sapiens.*

Most persons react favorably to harmonious conditions, keeping in mind that harmony is a relative term and that, generally speaking, one person's harmony may be another person's discord. We are much happier in a pleasant environment. But what happens when something disturbs that pleasure? A job is lost, resulting in a dramatic drop in economic status. A nation's vital resources dwindle, causing panic buying and hoarding. We join a mystical organization, and some friends and acquaintances may become distant or shy away from us. Stress and pressure result.

It is in the midst of just such times as described above, and a host of other events, that we, as mystical students, should calmly stand outside of ourselves and take a broad, dispassionate view of our situation. At such a juncture in our lives we should ask ourselves: "Am I a Human Barometer?" We should probe deeply into ourselves in an attempt to find that place where true happiness and security lies. Do we enjoy a relatively *high* barometric pressure rating, resulting in sunny skies, because of our good job, our many possessions, our loving family? Or do we experience a *low* in pressure, causing clouds and rain, because of the loss of any one of the above sunny conditions?

A rational mystical organization will not advocate that its members attempt a stoic philosophy of life. It is unrealistic to expect that a human being will look upon personal disasters with complete indifference. We will feel the pressure; we will experience the emotions and storms as long as we dwell within a physical body. Students of mysticism, however, should be attempting to forge within themselves a permanent anchor. Through their studies, their special exercises, and resultant inner unfoldment, a certain *link* with the Divine Mind will grow stronger.

A secure bedrock, true happiness, and relative imperturbability in life definitely should not be totally dependent upon one's income, friends, family, politics, or social standing. All such ties are unreliable and impermanent.

In reply to our original question, we are better able to cope with life's pressures by utilizing the higher attributes and faculties of the Supreme Intelligence resident within our beings. In doing so, we will be far less apt to resemble a barometric indicator of chaotic conditions.

We also suggest that students take a much higher perspective on life in general. By that we mean at the time of so-called death, the soul personality will not take with it any of the evanescent physical conditions about which we have spoken. What will *accompany* us into the cosmic realms is the level to which we have attained attunement, establishing that link with the Mind of God.

If, for example, we find ourselves suddenly off balance because of a dramatic shift in our nation's politics, or a fire in our home, or a flare-up of anger between family members, or for some other reason, we strongly urge mystical students not to lose sight of the larger picture of life. We can mentally step back and ask our higher self within: How can I constructively change this situation or how can I change myself for the better? For further example, if we should fall ill, we begin searching for the *cause* of illness and then work toward a more balanced physical level of health.

In other words, during times of stress and tension, it is more important than ever to utilize these higher faculties resident within the human system in order to achieve stability. Yes, we do feel the pressure. Yes, we do struggle with our emotional nature. It is wrong to assume that a person will not be affected in some manner by painful trials in life.

But we do not allow passing troubles to run rampant over us. If our situation is unsatisfactory, we begin mentally creating, *visualizing*, a more agreeable state of affairs. We reach deep within ourselves for contact with that anchor, that stronghold, where peace and harmony reign supreme at all times.

It would be constructive for the mystical student to consider reading well-written historical novels that deal with true events. The book might focus either on a particular personality or on the sweep of events in a certain country. This is suggested so that we will gain a clear realization of the fact that history often *repeats* itself. We may then come to realize the foolishness of emotional over-reactions to national and local problems, and we will also come to appreciate how other mystically minded persons of the past dealt with similar events and crises in their lives.

By refusing to become a human barometer in these stressful times, by establishing a stronger connection within ourselves, and by utilizing the higher faculties of mind as often as possible, we have noted that sincere mystical students are, in general, calmer individuals. Their mental and spiritual well-being seems to be above average to superior.

This reminds me of a relevant paragraph found in the excellent collection of inspirational writings entitled *Unto Thee I Grant:*

Their pleasures are moderate, and therefore they endure; their repose is short, but sound and undisturbed. Their blood is pure; their minds are serene, and the physician findeth not the way to their habitations.

"What causes us to choose

one path over another?

What influences the decisions,

the choices we make?"

Chapter 11

Are We Free?

"Do we live according to a cosmic plan or are we free to do what we want to do?" It may very well be that since the dawn of self-consciousness and the emergence of the belief in a Supreme Being, humanity has been attempting to either evade the laws of nature that govern us all or has been seeking ways to act in harmony with them.

The eternal wrestling with such burning questions as, "Am I free or am I a slave to fate?" has not been the exclusive province of ancient philosophers and wandering mystics. Many persons today see the dual concepts of release and restraint as constituting two pathways, one of which they assume we must choose in order to enjoy peace of mind.

The path of *release*, on the one hand, is often reflected in humanity's desire for fewer government regulations on all levels involving an effort to disentangle self from an alleged maze of fixed laws to which one may feel unnecessarily bound. Further, some persons feel they are needlessly restricted by the prevailing moral code of the society in which they live, and they may even resort to lavish or licentious behavior in order to demonstrate their emancipation.

The latter example is well represented in the dramatic poem *Faust,* by Johann Wolfgang von Goethe. This is the tragic story of a learned doctor who, tormented by a sense of physical and spiritual dissatisfaction, and realizing the limitations of human knowledge, barters his soul to Mephistopheles in exchange for worldly experience and great power. As the allegorical tale unfolds, it becomes abundantly clear that he has merely exchanged one set of symbolic restrictions upon himself for another.

The path of *restriction*, on the other hand, asserts that humanity is better off when it is almost totally suppressed. We are all aware that from time to time there arises from the vast sea of humanity a tyrant who in some manner seizes great power and weaves a pattern of virtual imprisonment of his people. This severe restriction may take the form of a simple crushing of opposing voices and the abolition of constitutional guarantees. Dictatorship may also cloak itself in the form of an imposition of a great network of rules so all-encompassing as to choke off personal initiative and creativity. However, the thirst for freedom on the part of the greater populace inevitably bursts forth with sometimes extremely unfortunate consequences for the tyrant.

Some mystical students feel that the austere life of a hermit or anchorite will lead to spiritual enlightenment. This too is another manifestation of an adherence to the path of restriction.

When dealing with social precepts, moral codes, and mysticism, the soul personality appears to resist the extremes of absolute slavery and absolute freedom. There seems to be the innate inclination on the part of the Inner Self to be both partially bound to some form of law or regulation and, at the same time, to be relatively free of rigid domination.

Beginning at birth—and perhaps even before birth—we are not, and cannot be, absolutely free. For example, there is nothing to be done about certain definite conditions of our birth. Once we are born we do not have a choice as to whom our parents are, what our race is, where our country of origin is located, and a host of other conditions. It is postulated by some that the soul personality before birth is attracted to a set of parents and a situation (call it raw material) that will afford the soul personality the opportunity to unfold further.

In his book *Mansions of the Soul*, H. Spencer Lewis puts the discussion into clear perspective with this viewpoint:

> *When the Soul enters the physical body, it takes residence within a physical form prepared, in purity or contamination, to receive it. The physical form has no choice in the selection of the Soul to be its companion through the forthcoming cycle of existence. The Soul, on the other hand, has no free choice in the*

selection of the body in which it is to be imprisoned or glorified for another period of incarnation. Both are drawn together, attracted to each other, and united by the Law of Compensation—the law of justice.

As the child develops and grows closer to adulthood, more far-reaching decisions begin to be made. We choose a career in life, and then perhaps we change our minds. We decide upon a religion or philosophy to guide us and, again, perhaps we change that too. We exercise some measure of freedom in choosing where to live, whom to marry, what to wear, and so on. But regardless of the social position or political power we attain in our mundane lives, there still remain those elements in life over which we exercise little or no control.

Anyone who has found himself or herself at the mercy of a hurricane, tornado, or great earthquake knows very well that humanity at that point is like a teacup attempting to hold the ocean. And the most ruthless tyrants the world has ever known have not yet been able to control the silent thoughts of other people.

We spoke earlier of the concept of life's two pathways: release and restraint. We feel that humanity is neither free nor enslaved. The truth of our condition here on earth seems to lie somewhere in between. Therefore, we should now look upon these two pathways as being two polarities of a single avenue that we will call the *pathway of consciousness*. Allow us to further substitute the words *freedom* and *restraint* and instead ask the question whether we shall move forward or remain stagnant along our pathway of consciousness—on our journey toward greater inner development.

To illustrate the above concept, let us suppose that the soul personality, proceeding smoothly along this mystical path, is suddenly confronted with an obstacle to its progress. The personality strongly desires to continue its forward movement. But the obstacle—whether a powerful personality or an alluring material possession—is very distracting, and we are tempted to be diverted from our progress toward our goal. As a result, a fierce battle rages within the cauldron of the mind. A decision must be made as to whether one should continue forward movement or remain behind.

In such cases we are either free or bound only insofar as to the type of decision we make. No one on earth is immune from the necessity of eventually having to make difficult choices along life's journey. So, it appears as though we are free only insofar as the choices we make in life. But, what causes us to choose one path over another? What influences the decisions, the choices we make?

Traditional mystical teachings assert that the nature of the cosmic force itself is beneficial and constructive. It also postulates that this Cosmic is the directing Mind permeating everything, everywhere. This sacred Intelligence, or Soul, becomes conscious of itself upon the birth of the child.

When the outer consciousness of the mystical student is in full attunement with this Soul, a divine afflatus takes place. We then receive some form of knowledge, and we experience as well a measure of emotional upliftment. We are thereafter strongly *inclined* to follow as closely as possible a higher way that has been revealed to us. Although the experience itself may be quite fleeting and of only a small degree of intensity, there is a definite elevation of consciousness. Subtle changes for the better eventually begin to filter through the human organism and manifest themselves in the personality. One such subtle change is the tendency toward following higher impulses, or *guidance*, if you will, of this Mind deep within us.

On our pathway of consciousness, we are not directed by predestination or dominated by fate; we are free to either move ahead or to stagnate. The governing motive behind our decision, one way or the other, is the strength of either some lower or higher impulse.

However, there is the danger of taking drastic action, of going to extremes. We spoke earlier in this discussion of those who either abandon their moral codes completely or who resort to the ascetic life of a hermit. In our desire to follow the higher impulse, awakened by our mystical experiences, we may forget that we do live in a physical body and that its needs must be met in a balanced way.

An early Rosicrucian pamphlet had this to say about unseen influences:

> We believe, in fact we know, that there is a Divine Intelligence, a moving actuating mind in the universe. We know that this governing Intelligence directs the order of the universe, not according to whim and fancy, but according to a stupendous system of natural law that is just, because it manifests equally for all beings. We know that the human mind, the cosmic part of our being, is the controlling factor in directing the influences that these laws exert. We may attune ourselves at times directly with the source of the soul power in the cosmic realm and receive an influx of added strength, inspiration, and divine guidance.

Dear reader, as a special exercise, when you are able to do so, separate yourself from all worldly distractions, and then go into your most private and sacred chamber of meditation. When you feel you have achieved a deeply satisfying sense of inner attunement, make a clear and strong suggestion to your higher self that henceforth, in all your major thoughts, plans, and decisions in life, you will be more readily inspired and moved by divine impulses. Thus, in future actions, you will sense that you are freely choosing the higher Path where your motives are in harmony with your conscience and with the Mind of God.

"The student who is temperate is likely to attract others who ask what philosophy of life is being followed that brings about such serenity and peace of mind."

Chapter 12

Setting a Good Example

"What is the best way to impress others with the practical value of authentic mystical teachings?" The best instructor is one who sets a good example in his or her daily life. Having said that, however, we should also realize that there is a considerable diversity in the personalities of the students. Each student is ideally, to one degree or another, attempting to unfold the personality and to improve self. Each one, moreover, regularly faces a different domestic and/or business situation. Membership in the Rosicrucian Order, for example, reflects a broad spectrum of educational, religious, and philosophical learning and understanding.

We mention this broad range of students because one of the chief aims of the Order is for each student to eventually formulate a personal philosophy of life, one that will mirror at any given time the student's highest degree of personal mastery. Therefore, each member proceeds along the mystical path in accordance with an individual level of understanding and unfoldment. The example each student sets or exhibits to the world will be representative of that person's stage of overall development.

Let us take a few moments here to briefly clarify what the difference is between being an *example* of something and being a *sample* of something. An example is a "particular single item, fact, incident, or aspect that may be taken as fairly typical or representative of all of a group or type." An example is something that is characteristic of a person, place, or product, and may be used as a model.

A sample, on the other hand, may be likened to a cut of cloth that is taken from a large roll. It is exactly the same as the original. For instance, many orchestras may play Beethoven's *Fifth Symphony*, and any part of that symphony is a sample of the whole symphony. On the other hand, any Beethoven symphony may be looked upon as a good example of the larger category known as *classical music*.

We mention all of this, because in life we may gain inspiration from people we respect and perhaps strive to emulate. In other words, we may desire to be exactly like the original. However, in this desire to imitate, there is both a negative and a positive element. Many years ago, a very powerful and unusual stage and screen actor attained great prominence in North America. Thereafter, there arose in his wake literally dozens of performers who seemed to be trying their best to imitate his manner of speaking and characterization. As a result of such attempted duplications, none of the copies were able to be accorded the high critical praise the original consistently received.

Continuing
of the performing
singer who freely
and knowledge abo
who preceded him.
while on tour with th
spent his spare time
and supported the vo
learned more from tha
The young man has long   ....ish himself in
his own right, expressing ... unique personality.

the tired old cliché:
you rich?" It is h
fixed in min
teaching
poss

In other words, the young man never attempted to be
a mere duplication of the original. And neither should we,
as serious students of mysticism, attempt to force ourselves
into a preset mold. You may want to explain to family
and friends that true students of mysticism do not seek
to think and act exactly alike. Rather, as we said before,
each is encouraged to ultimately develop his or her own
personal philosophy in accordance with each individual's
mystical growth and understanding.

Now that we have a clearer idea of the difference
between being a good example as opposed to being an exact
copy, perhaps it would be well to interject at this point
that one does not have to be extremely wealthy or indulge
in a conspicuous display of riches and ornamentation to
be a good example of a successful student. We often hear

Well, if you're so smart, why aren't
...ped that each student will keep it firmly
... that the primary goal of any true mystical
... is not to bring about an accumulation of material
...ssions.

On the one hand, we want to stress that there is absolutely nothing wrong with having in your possession a good measure of the world's riches. On the other hand, it is in the everyday *use* of these things where the critical problems normally arise. Some persons allow themselves to become captives of their own prosperity—they have permitted material things to become their master, rather than striving to become the absolute master of their material world.

Returning to the subject of setting a good example, we also suggest the student point out to those who wish to know what material benefit philosophical studies can possibly give them—seeing as how the student himself or herself may be in relatively moderate circumstances—that the refinement of character and unfoldment of the inner self does not necessarily bring about material wealth. Comprehensive mystical teachings generally attempt to improve all three levels of self: the physical, the mental, and the spiritual. As each student gains in self-knowledge and self-mastery, perhaps there will indeed manifest a concurrent rise in one's worldly material status. Remember, however, such a benefit is purely incidental and is not of first concern to the mission of authentic mystery schools.

As another brief sidelight, it is rather amusing to witness those who scoff at any mystical teachings that promote self-improvement and the elevation of consciousness, while they themselves will regularly spend many hundreds and perhaps many thousands of dollars on all sorts of amusements and games. In fact, such persons may expend a *great deal* more on amusements than mystical students do on their annual dues and donations. Yet, what material value and gain have the amusement-seekers attained at the end of a given year? We have no quarrel at all with life's amusements; such is necessary to maintain a mental balance. However, it is a rather poor argument to accuse mystical students of wasting time and money, while at the same time pouring huge amounts of currency into entertainment and games on a daily basis.

The whole discussion of example setting can get into even more rarified and abstract considerations. For instance, an example may be a *representative reaction*, which follows a pattern or series of events. Such a reaction will then tend to either encourage or discourage the average person. To explain, let us suppose that people who purchased a certain brand of automobile found that they experienced serious engine problems after several years. Consumers would eventually see that automobile maker as setting a poor example of automobile manufacturing standards.

Conversely, it is a self-evident truth that the world loves a producer of goods that consistently reflect high quality of workmanship. Such a producer is always pointed out as setting a *good example* of reliable manufacturing standards.

Let us now consider a few general guidelines that we trust will be of some help in an attempt to be a good example of a student of mysticism in everyday life:

• Control any tendency to be *overbearing* to others about your studies. Super salespeople are fine under certain conditions, but in our case others may diplomatically agree with us, be polite with us, in order to be rid of our incessant pressure. It is counterproductive to have others forcefully smiling while we badger them about the error in their thinking. Allow others to have their say as well. Be understanding and tolerant with anyone who is sincerely living according to a philosophy that gives them a measure of peace and satisfaction. When it comes time for the mystical student to express his or her views, do so with conviction and strength, but never from a standpoint of condescension or disapproval of others' reasonable beliefs.

- In the area of ingesting food and drink, and in the overall indulgence in the physical pleasures of life, avoid extremes. A mystical student who is moderate in approach to these things finds that the physical body will function more harmoniously. A total denial of pleasure, or a wildly abandoned enjoyment, can bring about many psychological and physical ills. The student who is temperate is likely to attract others who ask what philosophy of life is being followed that brings about such serenity and peace of mind.

- Be supportive of the arts and other activities reflective of the finer things of life. Praise good and uplifting creations and downplay any tendency toward destructive criticism. There is wisdom in the admonition someone once gave regarding remaining silent if we cannot find something positive to say about a situation. Help those causes that strive to elevate humanity. If you do not have the wherewithal, for example, to purchase fine art, or the time to attend great performances, then at least speak well of them, praise them, when the occasion arises.

- Try to be as conversant as possible with the teachings and viewpoints of your studies. If, for example, someone asks, "what do the Rosicrucians think" with regard to some mystical topic, answer fully and completely. The primary restriction with respect to the privacy of the teachings of some organizations lies in the fact that they do not wish to have nonmembers reading their lessons. If a person is interested enough, he or she may simply make application for membership. Meanwhile, Rosicrucian students can certainly discuss their philosophy with their friends and family. Therefore, be open and responsive. Others will appreciate an honest answer, plainly given. In fact, it may well inspire them to seek to know more about the teachings.

• Continue to practice the mystical exercises and experiments. Remain open to knowledge so that you may continue the slow and gradual evolution of your soul personality. Regularity of contemplation and meditation will assist in the unfoldment process and may subtly *attract* those persons who are silently seeking that which others have already found. Follow the wise guidance and counsel of the soul of God within you.

If you wish to be a good example on behalf of that which you truly believe in, let us again recall the excellent advice given in *Hamlet*:

This above all: to thine own self be true,
And it must follow, as the night the day,
Thou canst not then be false to any man.

"Cowards die many
times before their deaths;
The valiant never taste
of death but once."

Chapter 13

Are You Prepared for Transition?

"Recently I witnessed the passing away of a dear relative, and I have noted within myself a growing fear of sudden death. How do I begin to overcome this feeling?"

Of the two major portals in life, birth and death, so-called death seems to be the one that causes the greatest amount of anxiety. The dread that all the good things we enjoy here on the material plane will suddenly and ruthlessly be taken away may very well cause the welling up within of a possible phobia concerning life's end. To such a person, it often seems unfair, arbitrary, and callous that such a thing should occur. Nor is one able to fight back at such a time, for death seems to be a massive force that simply moves in and takes one away to a distant place, never to return.

Poetry has been written, songs composed, and stories authored concerning the fear of death and its aftermath. No one has drawn a better portrait of such terror than Shakespeare, when he has one character in the play *Measure for Measure* cry out:

Ay, but to die, and go we know not where;
To lie in cold obstruction, and to rot;
This sensible warm motion to become
A kneaded clod; and the delighted spirit
To bathe in fiery floods or to reside
In thrilling regions of thick-ribbed ice;
To be imprison'd in the viewless winds,
And blown with restless violence round about
The pendent world; . . . 'tis too horrible!
The weariest and most loathed worldly life
That age, ache, penury, and imprisonment
Can lay on nature is a paradise
To what we fear of death.

How or why the generality of humanity formulated such a repulsion of life's end, and decided it was an ugly experience, can only be conjectured upon at this point. Unfortunately, the hierarchies of some strict religions today find it in their best interests to continue feeding those fears and warn of an unpleasant experience which awaits the evildoer. These religions have actually borrowed such a concept from much earlier beliefs and made it part of their current philosophy.

For example, in the famous reconstruction of an ancient rock tomb in the Rosicrucian Egyptian Museum in San Jose, California, will be found a striking wall painting known as *The Scale of Judgment*. The painting depicts a person who has departed life and is now being escorted through the underworld by the jackal-headed god

Anubis. At one point, the traveler has his heart weighed on the scale of judgment. If his heart is *heavy* with negative karma, he is then given over to a ferocious-looking creature who proceeds to devour the luckless wanderer. If his heart, on the other hand, is as *light* as a feather, he is permitted to enter the divine presence of the great god Osiris.

We can freely speculate that such a concept may very well have been the prototype of the much later *salvation* religions.

Serious mystical teachings look upon the end of life as a *separation* of the two primary aspects of our beings: body and soul. We see the body, with its blood, bone, and tissue, as being a great mass of physical cells that have a radiating atomic structure. However, within the nucleus of each cell there is that inanimate, intangible soul and life force which entered the body with the first breath and departs with the last. If we can imagine the two conditions collectively, physical and nonphysical, in the form of a duality, we will better understand their eventual *separation*. In other words, it is well to remember that we have two bodies, the physical and the psychic.

The two forces combined tend to radiate and pulsate, creating what is commonly called the *aura*, surrounding the body. These two forces, at certain stages of mystical activity, can seem to separate without causing a final passing away of consciousness. Many mystical students know this temporary separation as *astral* or *psychic projection*. Of course, the term *separation*, when used regarding psychic projection, is another misnomer, as is the term "death." The projected psychic body is always connected to the physical body and cannot be severed except by final *transition*.

We say that death is an incorrect name because neither the physical body nor the psychic body ever ceases to exist. In both cases they return to their more basic forms of existence. Therefore, we much prefer the term transition, as what does occur is actually in the form of a change, a shift, a transfer of position from one state of continued existence to another.

If we may use the analogy of a full glass of water as constituting our living bodies, we will see that the pouring away of the water (representing the soul and life force) in no way destroys the water itself nor does it blot out and extinguish the glass. Each continues in its own way until the two are united once again for a common purpose.

The subjects of karma and reincarnation are covered in other sections of this book, and therefore we will confine our discussion to the anticipation of transition. According to our viewpoint, the soul personality experiences life's gradations of emotions only while located in the physical body. This accounts for the gamut of happiness people experience while in a "near death" situation. As long as there is that connection between the physical and the psychic bodies there is the likelihood of an emotional response, due to the intricate web of the two nervous systems and brain activity. However, the encounters or events that take place on the much higher *cosmic* plane after transition can only be speculated upon at this time.

As far as conscious awareness of life after transition is concerned, we might use the analogy of a person who falls asleep, does not dream all night, and then awakens the next morning. The last thing he or she knew was relaxing in bed, preparing for sleep. The next conscious realization was awakening the next morning. There very well may have been many experiences during the interval, but a veil of forgetfulness of that unconscious interlude very often descends upon life's reawakening.

To carry the above example a bit further, the person who goes to sleep at night, loaded down with thoughts of the day's trials and tribulations, can *plan ahead* for the next day. He or she may be suffering the ill effects, for example, of a violent temper and may sincerely desire to encounter life's problems in a more mature and rational way. For further example, he or she may have difficulty meeting the proper responsibilities of life and a tendency toward procrastination. Such persons may strongly want another chance to conquer their weaknesses and forge ahead to higher goals. A new day offers such a chance.

In other words, transition does not bring with it eternal suffering, nor does it carry forward endless amusement. It is a doorway to opportunity, an initiatory portal of hope, and a gateway toward eventual peaceful reconciliation with self and with the greater Cosmic Mind.

It is well for the student of mysticism to also keep in mind what is stressed in rational teachings: transition is a natural part of our lives and ultimately cannot be avoided by anyone. One insightful humorist pointed out the inclination of many of us when he stated that some people are secretly hoping that at the moment of their passing away, a doctor will rush into their presence with a newly discovered magic elixir that will indefinitely prolong life.

On the other hand, if we may turn our attention briefly again to Shakespeare, we will find in this brief passage from *Julius Caesar* a calm and stately look at transition:

> *Cowards die many times before their deaths;*
> *The valiant never taste of death but once.*
> *Of all the wonders that I yet have heard,*
> *It seems to me most strange that men should fear;*
> *Seeing that death, a necessary end,*
> *Will come when it will come.*

With respect to our preparation for this natural event called transition, we have normally suggested that the student try to leave behind an orderly situation for others to deal with. A legal will should be prepared. This is not an attempt on our part to be morbid or unduly blunt, but we are simply pointing out the fact of the inevitable transition of every person now living on earth. We may each have cherished dreams of our loved ones receiving our worldly goods after we depart; but if a legal will is not in place, the recipients may be those whom we least wish to receive our possessions. Furthermore, if we are leaving a large variety of items behind, it becomes a burden upon others to decide what to do or guess what the departed may have had in mind. The preparing of a will is one practical way of realistically facing transition.

Next, try to *visualize* your final passing as being one of brief duration, free of prolonged suffering and strife. Also, those whom we deeply love in this life, and desire to be near, may very well be attracted to us in the next incarnation. The fact that we may not recall our former life doesn't negate the fact that we may be able to achieve further happiness and contentment, in the presence of loved ones, if we plan ahead now.

Finally, prepare for transition by steadily working toward spiritual growth in this life. Sound and sane mystical teachings can assist us to continue the gradual evolution of our higher faculties, with a clear conscience, which we can proudly offer up to our Creator when the time comes. Consider this concurrence, written by the Greek philosopher Epictetus:

> *If Death surprise me . . . it is enough if I can stretch forth my hands to God and say, "The faculties which I received at Thy hands for apprehending Thine Administration, I have not neglected. I have done Thee no dishonor. Behold how I have used the senses which Thou gavest me. Take them back and place them wherever Thou wilt! They were all Thine, Thou gavest them me." If man depart thus minded, is it not enough? What life is more noble, what end happier than this?*

"Somewhere along life's highway, we gain an insight into the very nature of the God within."

Chapter 14

Thoughts About Reincarnation

"I have an intense interest in the subject of reincarnation. Any discussion about it would be appreciated." Reincarnation is in fact one of those subjects that appears to hold a consistent fascination for students deeply interested in mysticism and often even for those who cannot be classified as true seekers. Sometimes the popularity of this subject rises to a higher level among the general populace when an eminent personality publicly discloses a personal concurrence with the doctrine of rebirth.

No matter how often one may hear it stated in a Rosicrucian discussion group or read it in an official lecture, it is best to stress the fact that AMORC does not present the subject of reincarnation to its students as being a fact. In an early lesson it is stated plainly that ". . . our intent is not to convince you of the validity of the law of reincarnation." It is basically offered as a logical theory that can only be definitely proven as a result of a personal experience had by the student. There is wisdom in the old saying: "A man convinced against his will is of the same opinion still."

Until the individual has realized within his or her consciousness a personal truth of reincarnation, it must remain in the realm of speculation. There are many serious students of mysticism who have not yet had that inspiring realization of a personal truth of reincarnation, yet they are intellectually convinced of its existence because of the sheer logic of the explanations given. On the other hand, there are those who do not accept it for various reasons, but who continue their studies while laying the subject aside for the time being.

H. Spencer Lewis, in his classic publication *Mansions of the Soul*, had this to say about reincarnation:

> *Whether one believes in or accepts the doctrine of reincarnation or rejects it, the truth of the principles will continue to manifest itself and the laws will continue to operate. We neither obliterate nor modify a law or principle by denying it or refusing to accept it. Therefore, it behooves everyone to become acquainted with the facts and at least to know something of the laws under which we are living, and by which we are directed and controlled in our existence.*

We are reminded of the old discussion concerning worldly attainment as opposed to spiritual attainment. If reincarnation is true, just what is carried over from one life to another? We have found it extremely interesting how often certain people will claim to be the reincarnation of the same famous past personality. Just why some individuals insist on being known as the reincarnation of Cleopatra or Alexander the Great, for example, we must leave to the reader's imagination.

The point is that these people may feel that the worldly attainment of a Hannibal, for instance, is sufficient reason to assume that these past personalities were equally accomplished on the spiritual plane as well. However, worldly acclaim and material accomplishment does not necessarily have anything at all to do with the inner spiritual level one has or has not attained. Moreover, it may very well have been the karmic situation of a past personality to experience the dizzy heights of worldly acclamation in order for certain painful lessons to be learned and personality problems to be overcome.

One has only to glance at the ocean of historical novels and biographical writings to realize that some of the people the world has called "great" were anything but that from a spiritual point of view. On the other hand, some personalities of the past, who strove in relative obscurity to improve the lot of humanity, and thereby enhance their own inner selves, are often either misunderstood or simply overlooked by the masses.

For example, if we examine some widely circulated encyclopedias, there we will still see propagated the old, biased histories of such noble personalities as the Egyptian Pharaoh Akhenaten and Count Alessandro Cagliostro. Even today the former is sometimes labeled as a "fanatic" while the latter is called a "charlatan." Meanwhile, the beauty and nobility of their soul personalities, plus the dramatic scope of their *real* work, are almost completely unknown, except to the serious student of mysticism.

If reincarnation is a fact, then once again, just precisely what is carried over from life to life? First let us state that the condition called the *storehouse of memory* remains with a personality forever. Moreover, this storehouse of memory, with its myriad forms of experience indelibly etched within the consciousness, is actually a basic ingredient constituting the personality itself. Further, the psychic level, to which the personality has attained, will remain at that certain level when the soul personality is ready for another existence.

In other words, the newly born child will retain the psychic and spiritual level of achievement from the end of its past lifetime. It is stated, moreover, that various strong desires for higher and constructive accomplishment will also be carried over. For example, one may return with the definite inclination to be a concert pianist; this being the burning desire at the end of the past life. Theoretically the child will then be attracted to ways and means of accomplishing that desire. It is also postulated that if a person were a murderer, robber, or engaged in brutal assaults upon others, then that person will *not* carry over the desire to continue such negative activity.

So, what is carried over? Basically, the intangibles of our lives: memories, experiences, talents, and inclinations, plus (most importantly) the spiritual plane of accomplishment.

Therefore, mystical students, in the midst of daily activities, should never let the thought be far from consciousness that they are steadily building up what amounts to higher *ideals*, knowing that these things are eternal and will not fade at the close of this span of existence.

Just how important is it for the student of mysticism to have a personal realization of reincarnation? How does this help a person in daily life? This is another one of those questions about which we will find strong opinions on either side. Some will take the position that it is totally unimportant whether or not one proves reincarnation to self. Others will state with equal force that one cannot fully realize mystical development unless such a realization is experienced. As indicated earlier, authentic teachings do not force students to accept reincarnation. They are encouraged to keep an open mind and not allow an attitude of intolerance to be present regarding the matter.

A person may in fact continue his or her unfoldment and not have a realization of reincarnation for years to come. Inner development is not curtailed because of such a question in the mind.

Perhaps the entire matter is a moot point because eventually many serious students of mysticism seem to have some sort of an experience with reincarnation as they faithfully practice the exercises and experiments. Such an experience, to one degree or another, automatically takes the whole question out of the realm of pure speculation and places it into the arena of an inner *truth*. At such a point, the student often takes the position that he or she knows it to be a personal truth regardless of whether the whole world denies the fact of reincarnation.

Another interesting question arises at this point: if we do reincarnate, will we ever stop reincarnating? Here we enter the field of inquiry concerning those whom (as the theory postulates) we assume have achieved that level of perfection whereby they reportedly no longer have a need for returning to the material plane. However, can we be absolutely certain that such spiritual masterminds do not return? Do we know beyond all doubt that one can in fact achieve such an exalted plane where he or she will not return? According to mystical tradition, the reason we continue to return to a physical body is so that we will learn various lessons, achieve higher goals, refine the personality, and accomplish a mastery of life. Does this negate the fact that a mastermind may come back to us, occasionally, to be of *service* to humankind?

Somewhere along life's highway, we gain an insight into the very nature of the God within. As these insights become more pronounced and definite, we slowly realize *who* and *why* we are. This gradual inward evolution reportedly brings about not a disgust and frustration with the world at large, but more of an appreciative sense of the harmony and beauty of life. The outer world begins to be a reflection of the light of one's expanding world within. Good cheer, a positive attitude, joy, and Peace Profound begin to reign in the heart and mind of such a developing mystic. Therefore, the thought of reincarnation becomes not an agonizing and horrible possibility, but one that is welcomed with open arms.

We feel it would be well for students on the Path to contemplate the words of one mystic who, when speaking of the soul's return, expressed her personal outlook on life. She said: "I love life. I enjoy it so much. I am happy to be learning and growing. I really hope I never have to stop unfolding my personality. I hope I will continue to reincarnate forever."

"Silence is healing to

the mind and body.

Our greater self is thus

given a chance to emerge,

to expand, to majestically reach

out in ecstasy and power."

Chapter 15

Silence

Silence appears to be a condition that, for the most part, humanity wants as little to do with as possible. The absence of constant chatter and assorted noises seems to create for people an irritating environment that they strive to correct in every possible way. To *enjoy* silence is looked upon by some as an odd pastime, one indulged in only by "mystics."

Peace and quiet are generally considered worthwhile for only an extremely brief period. Beyond that it is said to be a waste of time, as one should be doing "something interesting" instead. In fact, the desire of individuals for constant noise and frantic activity has given rise in our history to a method of punishment called the "Silent Treatment."

The Auburn System was a penal method of the 19th century in which inmates worked during the day and were kept in solitary confinement at night, with enforced silence at all times. The silent system evolved during the 1820s at Auburn Prison in Auburn, New York. Innovations designed to ensure strict silence included special seating arrangements at meals, greater extensions of the walls between the cells, and a rigid manner of marching with one's face toward a guard at all times.

In order to learn of an earlier use of silence, we travel further back into history. We find that among certain peoples, silence was used as a means of avoiding conflict and, at the same time, as a method of conducting needed business. The Greek historian Herodotus, who lived during the 5th century, B.C., spoke of a custom among the Carthaginians, and of people dwelling on the west coast of Africa, called Silent Trade. This was a specialized form of trade or barter in which goods were exchanged without audible communication and often without any meeting of the parties engaged in the transaction. Generally, one party went to a customary spot, deposited the commodities to be traded, and then withdrew, sometimes giving a signal such as a call or a gong stroke. Members of the other party then placed their articles and retreated. The first party returned, removing the second set of goods or allowing them to remain, until satisfactory additions were made. The second party then concluded the transaction by taking the original wares. As stated, this allowed for continued trade and avoidance of firsthand contact with strangers or hostile peoples.

Today, we find an offshoot of silent trade is often conducted, whereby an antagonistic nation will utilize the services of a third party to negotiate with another hostile nation, thereby avoiding physical confrontation and at the same time carrying forth the necessary transactions.

Thus far we have discussed how silence can be either a weapon used to subdue a people, or a useful tool used to bring about constructive results even at great odds.

The *love* of silence as a means of achieving mystical unfoldment found its advocates within the Roman Church. One example was in the person of one Miguel de Molinos, a Spanish priest of the 17th century. For Molinos, the way of Christian perfection was the interior way of contemplation to which anyone, with divine assistance, can attain. His doctrine, called *Quietism*, further held that perfection consists in passivity, or utter quiet of the soul, and in the suppression of human effort so that the divine action may have full play. The Quietistic element of silence and meditation later found its way into non-Christian movements through the centuries. Quietism appeared to advocate an extreme viewpoint with regard to outer, physical activities on a day-to-day level, and stressed instead passive meditation as the highest form of religious activity. A slur hurled at them by Papal critics at the time was the term *New Mystics*.

The conflict between Molinos' mystical religion and standard ecclesiastical authority went so far among the Jesuits that in the 17th and 18th centuries the Jesuits sometimes denied the very possibility of mystical experience. Quietism, with its lack of ostentation and rigid churchly formalities, became a subtle threat to the ruling

Papal hierarchy, which *insisted* on elaborate ritual. At any rate, Miguel de Molinos was finally condemned and sentenced to life in prison by Pope Innocent XI in 1687.

The recognition of the need for silence as an aid to mystical unfoldment found its way in religious circles in the United States in the form of the Quakers. The basic elements of Quietism run throughout Quakerism and emerge whenever "trust in the Inward Light" is stressed to the exclusion of everything else.

In our personal lives today, how often do we choose to speak when silence is the better way? Have not all of us gazed back over the pages of our private histories and wished that we had held our tongue at a particular moment? A mother denounces a son; a father rebukes his daughter; a husband insults his wife. Peace may reign thereafter, but in our silent remembering, that same denunciation, that same rebuke, that same insult may be dredged up from memory years later, and we recall it as evidence of our lack of love or understanding. We then desire most strenuously to turn back the pages of our lives and live that moment over again.

A practical mystical philosophy, however, would say that each day may bring new light and beneficial karma according to our actions now. One guideline might be that reflected in the philosophy of Antef, of the 19th century B.C., who said:

I am a silent man before a raging man and before a fool, in order to suppress wrath. I am calm, without hasty impulses, knowing what circumstances may arise, understanding possibilities of failure. I am a man who speaks in place where violence is normally applied, and I know when it is right for me to show anger.

Any sound guidelines for mastering life should include the control of unnecessary or negative utterances. Do not think that we *must* speak in all circumstances. The novelist Victor Hugo said: "A man is not idle because he is absorbed in thought; there is a visible labor, and there is an invisible labor."

Naturally, one may be an extremist one way or the other; however, to paraphrase an old bromide, it is true that if speaking is silver, then silence is golden. Moreover, we may express a great deal in very few words. A master of this technique was Calvin Coolidge, the laconic President of the United States. A story often related concerning his fame for brevity is as follows: President Coolidge was attending a dinner party, and a guest leaned over to him and said, "I have a bet with my friend here that I can get you to say more than two words." President Coolidge allegedly replied: "You lose."

As students of mysticism, we should realize that we are on earth in a dual body to enjoy the dual pleasures of life, and that to deny either the physical self its rightful joys and happiness or the spiritual self its spiritual pleasures is to make life unbalanced. We further maintain that through the wholesome joys and pleasures of life we add to the experiences that the soul personality is to have. We cannot get away from the fact that soul is within us for some purpose, and that purpose must be connected with the experiences of earthly life.

The soul is not in the body for the purpose of being imprisoned and made insensible; nothing would be gained by that. Further, the soul is incarnated in the flesh not to lessen the development of the personality, but to help in that unfoldment. Pleasures of the flesh and worldly experiences are not injurious or sinful to the physical body or the soul within.

However, we might well agree with the ancient mystics who warned us to be careful about the *dominating* desires of the material realm, to make sure that our lives are not totally selfish and beneficial only to the flesh. For there is that hunger, ambition, urge, and longing for many things on the part of the inner self. What we should be attempting to do is to build a balanced condition between body and soul, between the earth and the Cosmic. Silent attunement with the Cosmic is one way to do this. When all of the intelligence in the body is working in harmony and is evenly balanced, when there is full cooperation between the two realms, there is then the most ideal condition.

So, in silence and peace, we listen within. Through the soul, through inspiration, we learn the greatest lessons. These lessons are truth, for they do not come from the human mind. For the majority, the great trouble has been that human beings in their egotism do not listen to their conscience and unfortunately find no time for silent concentration and attunement.

Practical mystics can and should do this. In the privacy of our homes, during a quiet interval of study and reflection, we can attune ourselves with the Supreme Architect of the Universe. We are thus open to uplifting concepts, to divine inspiration. What comes to us at that time, what emotionally moves us, what we think, and what thoughts we receive and send forth at that time are effective for good and constructive purposes. If we hold negative thoughts, we will break the attunement.

To conclude, ideally we should create an environment that is free from personal strife, where there is relative peace or at least an absence of continuing harsh noises. Seek serenity and tranquility. Silence is healing to the mind and body. Our greater self is thus given a chance to emerge, to expand, to majestically reach out in ecstasy and power.

To quote the 14th century German mystic Johannes Tauler:

We honor and glorify Thy unspeakable mystery
With holy reverence and silence.

Index

The Rosicrucian Order, AMORC
Purpose and Work of the Order

The Rosicrucian Order, AMORC, is a philosophical and initiatic tradition. As students progress in their studies, they are initiated into the next level or degree.

Rosicrucians are men and women around the world who study the laws of nature in order to live in harmony with them. Individuals study the Rosicrucians lessons in the privacy of their own homes on subjects such as the nature of the soul, developing intuition, classical Greek philosophy, energy centers in the body, and self-healing techniques.

The Rosicrucian tradition encourages each student to discover the wisdom, compassion, strength, and peace that already reside within each of us.

www.rosicrucian.org

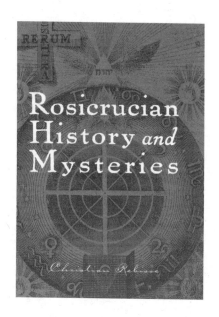

Rosicrucian History and Mysteries

by Rosicrucian author
Christian Rebisse

Softcover, 7.5 in. x 10.5 in.
244 pages

Suggested retail price: $24.95

Here is the definitive history of Rosicrucianism, from the earliest of times to the present. This book is a "must-read" for anyone interested in the Rosicrucian Order. This scholarly work is now available in English. This book is well researched—complete with endnotes, an index, a chronology, and a thematic bibliography suggesting sources for further reading. *Rosicrucian History and Mysteries* is abundantly illustrated with over 90 illustrations—many from rare and unusual sources. Your Rosicrucian library will not be complete without this exceptional volume.

For other books published by the Rosicrucian Order, AMORC, please visit www.rosicrucian.org

Treasures of the Rosicrucian Egyptian Museum

A Catalogue

by *Lisa Schwappach-Shirriff, M.A.*
Curator
Rosicrucian Egyptian Museum

Softcover, 7.5 in. x 10.5 in.
160 pages; color

Suggested retail price: $24.95

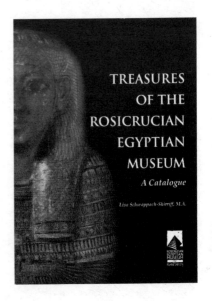

The history of the Rosicrucian Egyptian Museum in San Jose, California, began with a dream. H. Spencer Lewis, the leader of the museum's sponsoring organization, the Rosicrucian Order, AMORC, cherished this dream and through his efforts the museum came into being. Today, the Rosicrucian Egyptian Museum houses the largest collection of Egyptian, Assyrian, and Babylonian artifacts on exhibit in western North America.

This catalogue features the museum's major artifacts, including more than 250 artifact photos in color. Also included are essays providing fascinating insights into the daily life and culture of the ancient Egyptians, and a history of the Rosicrucian Egyptian Museum and its magnificent collection. With its captivating essays and beautiful photos, this museum catalogue brings ancient Egypt to life!

For other books published by the Rosicrucian Order, AMORC, please visit www.rosicrucian.org. *And for more information about the Rosicrucian Egyptian Museum, please visit* www.egyptianmuseum.org